Samuel F. B. Morse

Artist with a Message

by

John Hudson Tiner

illustrated by **Shirley Young**

**MOTT
MEDIA**

This book is dedicated
to
William J. and Brooksie Stanley

COPYRIGHT © 1987 by Mott Media, Inc.

Kurt Dietsch, Cover Artist

LIBRARY OF CONGRESS CATALOGING IN PUBLICATION DATA

Tiner, John Hudson, 1944—
    Samuel F. B. Morse: Artist with a Message

    (The Sowers Series)
    Bibliography: p. 165
    Includes index.

    SUMMARY: A biography of the artist and inventor who devised
the world's first practical telegraph system.
    1. Morse, Samuel Finley Breese, 1791-1872—Juvenile literature.
2. Artists—United States—Biography—Juvenile literature. 3.
Inventors—United States—Juvenile literature. [1. Morse, Samuel
Finley Breese, 1791-1872. 2. Inventors. 3. Artists] I. Young, Shirley,
ill. II. Title. III. Series: Sowers.

N6537.M66T56 1987   621.382'092'4 [B] [92]   87-61023
ISBN 0-88062-137-0

CONTENTS

1

The Secret Ambition

Nancy Shepherd said, "Give me your hand, Samuel. I'll walk you to school."

"I can go to Ma'am Rand's school by myself," Samuel Morse said.

"Your father instructed me to make certain you arrive on time," Nancy said. "Come along now and don't dawdle." Firmly she took his hand and led him along the street.

Samuel Morse quickened his steps to walk beside his nurse. "Can we walk along Breed's Hill? Maybe I'll find a musket ball like I did yesterday."

Nancy would have instantly refused any other request, but she enjoyed strolling along the top of the hill and telling her favorite stories about the town. However . . .

"No-o-o," Nancy said reluctantly. "Not today."

"Tell me about the Redcoats and patriots."

"Well, during the War of Independence the Red-coats fought the American patriots on Breed's Hill and on Bunker Hill," Nancy said. "During the

fighting, the enemy burned Charlestown to the
ground. But we drove the Redcoats out and rebuilt
Charlestown. The church meeting house where your
father preaches and the parsonage where you live were
two of the first buildings put back up.''

As she spoke her steps slowed, and soon she'd
forgotten all about walking Samuel to school. Instead
she told the stories she knew so well and pointed out
the sights.

''Charlestown is a small town,'' Nancy said, ''but
an important one. Along this road Paul Revere
galloped on his famous midnight ride to Lexington.
He sent a signal all the way from Boston to
Charlestown by lighting lanterns in the Old North
Church steeple.''

At length Nancy delivered Samuel to the kitchen
door of Ma'am Rand's home. Samuel walked in, late
again.

Ma'am Rand looked at him sternly. ''Samuel, say
'Pardon me' and take your seat,'' she said.

''Pardon me,'' Samuel said. He bowed stiffly, then
sat on the three-legged stool in front of the big stone
fireplace.

Ma'am Rand sat in the middle of her kitchen with
the students in a circle around her. An invalid who
seldom left her rocking chair, she governed her pupils
with a long rattan cane. She would reach across the
small room with her cane, hook a young culprit by
the collar, and pull him to his feet.

Today, classes started with reciting the alphabet.
Samuel knew the lesson well enough to chant his
alphabet along with the other students.

To Samuel's right was a chest of drawers, a bat-
tered piece of furniture with a cracked wax finish.
Samuel occupied his mind by imagining figures in the
network of cracks.

Why, that looked like Ma'am Rand's round face in the wood. Samuel pulled a straight pin from a nearby pin cushion and began tracing around the face. He forgot all about saying his lesson.

The face had no hair. Samuel scratched the wax with the pin to make Ma'am Rand's hair fluff out from under her bonnet. The face began to look more and more like her. Samuel stole a glance at the woman. Yes, he needed to add another line to show her double chin.

"Samuel Finley Breese Morse!" Ma'am Rand commanded. "Come here this instant! Look what you've done to the chest of drawers."

"I merely drew a picture."

"Young man, you draw on paper or canvas meant for that purpose. Give me the pin!" She took the pin and fastened Samuel by the end of his shirt to the skirt of her dress. "This will keep you out of trouble.

You're the pastor's firstborn son. He expects better things of you than scratching pictures on a chest of drawers!''

Dr. Jedediah Morse, Samuel's father, did expect great things from his son. Dr. Morse was a well-known figure in the Boston area. Every famous man who came to Boston came to see Dr. Morse. With obvious and honest pride, Dr. Morse would introduce Samuel as his firstborn son.

The visitors would ask Samuel, ''Young man, what will you do when you grow up? Will you become a minister like your father, or president of a college like your grandfather?''

''I don't know,'' Samuel would say.

''Maybe you'll write books like your father. His *Geography Made Easy* is the best geography book about America. Do you like to write?'' a man once asked.

''I . . . I like to draw.'' There! He'd said it. Now his father would know what he really wanted to do. ''I want to become an artist.''

Everyone laughed.

''Stuff and nonsense! Surely not, young man. Artists can't earn proper livings. They're hardly more than tramps and vagabonds. It's not a proper occupation for the son of a famous man.''

Dr. Morse said quickly, ''My son spoke in jest, of course.''

Samuel was not joking. As the months and years passed, he continued to be fascinated by drawing. But he kept his ambition a secret.

One day as Samuel and his brother, Sidney, were studying their homework assignments in their room, Samuel held up his slate. ''Sidney, what do you think of my picture of Mother?''

''It looks just like her,'' Sidney agreed. ''You're clever with your hands Samuel. You draw good portraits, but—''

"But what?"

"But Papa wouldn't like it."

"Why doesn't he like for me to draw pictures?" Samuel asked.

"People who want likenesses made of themselves are vain people."

"Vanity is a sin, I know," Samuel said, "but I'm not drawing a likeness of myself, I'm drawing one of Mother."

Sidney didn't argue. He went back to his studies, his head buried in a book, his lips moving as he memorized his lesson.

Dr. Morse stood in the doorway, silently observing his two sons at work. Samuel, unaware of his father's presence, continued to draw on the slate.

"Ahem. Have I not told you often," his father said in a slow even tone, "that making likenesses is a waste of precious moments?"

"Yes, sir," Samuel said hastily, erasing the picture.

"Did you finish your lessons?" Dr. Morse asked.

"Well enough," Samuel replied.

"Merely well enough? Quote it for me," Dr. Morse directed.

"Ah, 'All hope abandon, ye who enter here!' " Samuel quoted. "Ah . . . "

"Go on," his father prompted.

"Ah, 'All hope abandon, ye who enter here!' . . . I forget the rest," Samuel said miserably.

Dr. Morse turned to his other son. "Sidney, are you finished?"

"Yes," Sidney said. He closed the book and quoted, " 'I will talk of things heavenly, or things earthly; things mortal, or things evangelical; things sacred—' "

"I see you have your lesson well memorized, Sidney," Dr. Morse said. "Tell me, Samuel, why did you fail to memorize the story given to you?''

''I worked on other things,'' Samuel said.

Dr. Morse asked, ''Do you remember the fable of the hare and the tortoise?''

Samuel said, ''One day the two animals ran a race. The rabbit shot far in front. The turtle poked along. But the tortoise won, even though the hare was faster.''

''Why did he win?'' his father asked.

''Why, because the hare stopped too many times along the way to look at other things. He smelled the flowers, stopped to watch some ants work, and took a nap.''

''And the tortoise?''

''The tortoise kept plodding along. He wasn't turned aside by other matters, so he finished the race first.''

Dr. Morse put his arms around the two boys and pulled them closer. ''Samuel, you and Sidney remind me very much of the tortoise and hare. Sidney is like the tortoise. He is slow, but he moves forward steadily. He sets himself a goal and keeps going toward it until he reaches it.

''You, Samuel, are like the hare. You move swiftly. But you are distracted by other things and you forget the race. Take your drawing as an example. It is only a foolish whim which you will soon outgrow. In the meantime you could have been applying yourself to more useful matters.''

Dr. Morse arranged for Samuel to go off to boarding school when he was seven years old. He would attend Phillips Academy in Andover, a small town twenty-two miles north of Boston.

Dr. Morse had searched for the proper school for Samuel. ''It's the most respected school in the country. The Phillips family established the Academy with the goal to promote true piety and virtue in young scholars. Phillips will prepare you for your studies at Yale.''

On his last day at home, Nancy inspected Samuel critically before she let him go downstairs. ''Remember to be on your best behavior while you are with your father.''

''I will,'' Samuel promised.

After breakfast, he solemnly kissed Mother, hugged Nancy, and said goodbye to Sidney.

Sidney said, ''I'll miss you.''

''I'll write,'' Samuel promised Sidney. ''I'll use the secret ink. Only you and I will know how to read the message.''

Samuel composed his mind to be the dignified first-born son of Dr. Jedediah Morse. Being the oldest son of Dr. Morse was serious business and not to be taken lightly.

Outside the house, Dr. Morse waited in the carriage. He was a tall man, slender in build, his head thrust forward as if about to engage in earnest conversation. He dressed neatly and spoke in a mild but persuasive voice.

He could look so different from day to day. Most mornings he dressed in his long red gown and prepared his sermons in the upstairs study. On Sunday he faced the congregation in a black robe, white neck band, and powdered wig. Today, he looked more like a prosperous businessman.

''Good morning, Papa.''

''Good morning, Samuel,'' Dr. Morse said. ''Thank you, Nancy. You can attend to Sidney and Richard now. I'll take care of Samuel. Step lively, son. We've a great deal to do today. I must call on members of the congregation and visit the printer in Boston to pick up some books to take to Andover.''

"Why do you visit the people so often?" Samuel asked.

"A cold preacher makes a frozen congregation," Dr. Morse said. He clicked the reins and the horse obediently plodded into motion.

After running the errands, Dr. Morse delivered Samuel into the care of Mark Newman, the director of Phillips Academy.

When Samuel applied himself to his studies, he quickly rose to the head of the class, despite being one of the youngest students at the school. After a few months, however, other matters captured his imagination, and his grades suffered.

Samuel practiced his solo for the Exhibition Day assembly. Each year the Academy threw open its doors to welcome the families of the students. Each of the students played a small part in the assembly—recited a poem, sang in the choir, told a history story, and so on. Samuel was to sing a solo.

"*Oh, what can the matter be. . . .*" Samuel sang in practice.

Samuel Barrell, one of Samuel's three roommates asked, "Yes, Samuel, what can the matter be?"

Samuel stopped singing. "My grades," he said glumly. "Exhibition Day is only a week away and I'll never bring my grades high enough to be pleasing to Papa."

"Maybe he'll not come."

"Oh, he'll come. The Academy invited him to be the guest speaker."

The lunch bell sounded. "Let's eat, Samuel."

"Go ahead without me. I'll be along after I've finished my assignments."

Before opening his books, however, Samuel finished writing a letter to his brother. Using the secret ink he traced out two drawings at the bottom of the letter.

One showed a tortoise with its neck stuck out and its legs pumping furiously. The other one showed a hare lying on its back, its legs crossed and its eyes closed in daydreams. Under the hare he printed *SAMUEL*; under the tortoise he printed *SIDNEY*.

I'm not going to be a hare, Samuel told himself. Here at Andover, I'll settle down and . . . The ink on the paper dried and nearly disappeared from sight. He could barely make out the tortoise and the hare. Back in Charlestown, Sidney would heat the paper and the drawing would come back into view.

I wish I'd saved a copy of the picture, Samuel thought. I'll make a new one, but this time with the hare leaping over the tortoise as they reach the finish line!

Samuel pushed aside his books and began looking for drawing paper. He'd brought several sheets with him from home. Now they were all used.

Samuel picked up his quill pen and wrote to his

father: "Dear Papa, I hope you are well. Give my love to Mama and Nancy and my little brothers. Kiss them for me. Please, I will need some quills and some very good paper." He signed the letter Samuel Breese Morse, Your Son, 1799.

By the time he'd finished the letter, Samuel had missed the noonday meal. He didn't want to face his books on an empty stomach. He thought a minute, then picked up a pail. About a mile away, across the meadow behind the dormitory and into the woods, he'd found blackberry bushes along an old stone fence. He could eat all he wanted provided he picked his own.

Samuel closed the door, leaving his books behind—and unopened.

On the day of the Exhibition, people walked through the buildings and looked over samples of the boys' work hung on the classroom walls. Parents talked to the teachers to learn how well their children were actually doing.

Dr. Morse spoke to the entire assembly. He directed his words to the students. He spoke about life in two worlds, an earthly life and a heavenly one. "You are laying a foundation for both worlds," he told them. "The character and habits you are now forming will be likely to continue through this life, and to determine your future everlasting condition."

After the speech, Dr. Morse met with Mr. Foster, Samuel's teacher.

"Your son has been at the top of his class," Mr. Foster said.

"And now?" Dr. Morse asked. "I see none of his work on display."

"Ah, young Morse has eight demerits in spelling and eighteen for whispering. I'm afraid he spends his days dreaming while awake."

"How does he stand?" Dr. Morse asked.

"Samuel Morse is at the bottom of his class."

Dr. Morse turned to Samuel. "Come to the carriage with me," he said.

"Yes, Papa," Samuel said. Slowly, Samuel followed the solemn black-robed figure to the carriage underneath a maple tree. At least his father was kind enough to administer his tongue lashing away from the others in the privacy of the tree-lined drive.

In a surprisingly mild voice, Dr. Morse said, "Samuel, *you must learn to attend to one thing at a time.* It is impossible to do two things well at the same time."

Dr. Morse reached into his carriage and brought out a paper-wrapped package. "This," he said, "is a present for you from me."

Samuel could barely contain his relief. "Why, thank you, Papa. I didn't expect . . . I mean I know my grades are not their best." He tore open the package. Inside was a book, one he enjoyed reading, Plutarch's *Lives of Illustrious Men.*

Dr. Morse hugged his son. "Your mother has sent something of more immediate pleasure." He handed out a luncheon basket.

Samuel spread back the napkin. Inside were slices of meat, pieces of gingerbread, and a pie.

"Peach pie, I think," Dr. Morse said. "And Sidney sent a jug of his very own cider."

As they spread the picnic lunch, Dr. Morse said, "Mr. Foster says you dream while you are awake."

Samuel did not disagree.

"When you were born and proved to be a healthy youngster with the spark of genius in your eyes, your mother and I were full of pride. In fact, the pride frightened us."

"Why?" Samuel asked.

''We wondered, could we be too proud of our bright and healthy boy? Could we spoil you by too much love? I even spoke privately to a man whose opinion I trusted. He told us, 'Go ahead and love your boy.' And so we will. You are our dear son and whatever God's purpose is for you, it will show itself in its own good time and way.''

The next year Sidney, three years younger than Samuel, came to Andover to attend school.

Samuel studied as hard as his nature allowed. But it was Sidney who earned the best scores. Sidney, not Samuel, showed the promise of bringing honor to the Morse name.

When Samuel was thirteen he took an entrance test for Yale. Sidney, who was only ten, took the test, too, although he would not start at Yale right away. Dr. Timothy Dwight, the warm personal friend of Samuel's father and president of Yale, gave the test.

If Samuel passed he would be the youngest person in his class.

If he passed.

The examination began. Under the encouraging eyes of Dr. Dwight, the boys answered questions about Greek, Latin, and English grammar. Dr. Dwight posed problems in arithmetic and logic, and gave them compositions to write on historical subjects.

Finally, late in the afternoon, Dr. Dwight called a halt. ''I'll take the papers now,'' he said.

''When will we know the results?'' Samuel asked.

''In a day or so.''

To take his mind away from the test scores, Samuel volunteered to help around the house. He milked the cow, carried wood into the kitchen for Nancy, and took one of Dr. Morse's manuscripts across the toll bridge and into Boston to the printer.

Two days later Dr. Dwight announced the scores.

"Samuel, you passed, as did Sidney."

"When will I begin at Yale?"

"This fall," Dr. Dwight said. "Because of your brother's young age, he'll wait for another year before entering college."

During the summer before school started, Samuel secretly sketched the members of his family. He drew portraits of Papa, Mother, and his two brothers, Sidney and Richard. He planned to put the sketches together as a full-color family portrait.

Samuel Morse dreamed of being a great painter. Yet, except for the one slip as a young child, he'd never told anyone of his secret ambition. Somehow the time didn't seem right. Unfortunately, Samuel despaired of ever finding the proper time to reveal his plans for the future.

2

The Hill of Science

At Yale, Samuel Morse was a popular young man—six feet tall, courteous, and friendly. His classmates found him to be a good companion. They always received a warm welcome when they visited his room. They came to his room to watch his progress in drawing a flamboyant picture that took up most of one wall.

At first the drawing showed only a steep hill, labeled *The Hill of Science*, and stick figures of hapless students scrambling up it. Day by day the drawing grew. Samuel fleshed out the stick figures to be humorous portraits of his classmates.

Samuel Barrell, his roommate at Andover, also attended Yale, and they became college friends. Morse portrayed Barrell scrambling on his hands and knees in order to reach the summit. Joseph Dulles, another student, was sprinting in victory, almost to the top.

As the drawing neared completion, the students gathered to watch Samuel apply the finishing touches. He drew in Henry Ellsworth and John Bartlett as two poor fellows holding on to one another to stay on their feet.

Henry Ellsworth said, "Everyone's there but Morse. Where are you?"

Samuel Barrell said, "Look closely at the foot of the hill. See the sleepy-eyed individual? That's Morse!"

The figure struggled to crawl over a gigantic boulder blocking his path. The boulder was labeled *Dislike of Study*.

John Bartlett asked, "Can you paint my likeness?"

"I've not taken any lessons in painting," Morse admitted, "but I'll give it a try if you wish."

Morse drew the profile of John Bartlett on a small card, no more than three by four inches. With a precise hand, he inked in Bartlett's strong nose, plain face, and prominent sideburns.

Dissatisfied, Morse inspected his handiwork. "It looks rather lifeless." He found a fine brush and added color—pink flesh tones to the face and dark brown to the hair.

John Bartlett could not have been more pleased. "It's a most perfect likeness."

Morse said, "In that case, let me sign my name to it." He took the card and printed at the bottom in fine letters: *S. F. B. Morse*.

Soon other students asked for portraits to send home to their families. Morse did one for Joseph Dulles, showing the boy sadly overworked in his studies, one of Samuel Barrell, and even one of himself.

Morse showed himself as an artist, holding a brush in one hand and a palette in the other. He added a twinkle in his eyes as if he didn't quite take himself seriously.

But Samuel Morse was always thinking and always in action. To portray himself as a sleepy-eyed scholar who shunned study was not an accurate picture. His day at Yale began at five-thirty with morning prayers at the chapel, followed by a class, and then breakfast. During the day he studied, prepared for debates, and attended lectures. His day ended at eight o'clock at night with dinner and evening devotions.

Each Sunday, Dr. Timothy Dwight delivered a sermon in the chapel. He was a stocky man, with weak eyes, but an intense voice. He took a personal interest in the students. "I urge you," he said, "to learn to observe facts, and to use these facts in your own lives. An uneducated person can never become a good citizen."

Dr. Timothy Dwight was one of Samuel's favorite people at Yale. Later, when Dwight's eyes failed him, Samuel volunteered to read to him and act as his secretary.

Professor Jeremiah Day left his mark upon Samuel, too. He taught natural history. The students met in the Philosophical Chamber, a cold, unheated laboratory in the basement room of one of the solid, red-brick buildings. Despite the bleak surroundings, and being bundled against the cold, Jeremiah Day's enthusiasm for the subject set fire to the imagination of Samuel Morse.

In one experiment, Professor Day darkened the room and sent an electric current through a metal chain. In the darkness, the eerie blue glow danced along the links of the chain.

"As you know," Professor Day said, "Benjamin Franklin demonstrated that static electricity and lightning are the same although lightning is on a much grander scale. Franklin produced electricity by means of a static generator. Only seven years ago, in 1800, Alessandro Volta, an Italian scientist, invented the voltaic cell, the first steady supply of electric current.

The current can be made as powerful as one wishes by linking several cells in a series to make a Voltaic Pile, or battery.''

Professor Day connected wires to both sides of the battery. With a dramatic gesture, he slowly brought the ends of the wires together. Suddenly, a blue arc of electricity sparked across the gap, causing the students to jump in surprise. Professor Day pulled apart the wires and brought them together again. This time he held a piece of paper between the wires. Electricity sparked again, right through the paper.

''Look at the paper for yourself,'' Professor Day said.

Samuel Morse examined the hole in the paper. He marveled at how something without substance or form could actually punch a hole in the paper.

The demonstrations fascinated Samuel Morse. The next day, when class began, he asked, ''Electricity appears to be so mysterious and marvelous. Has anyone put it to use?''

''No,'' Professor Day said. ''Electricity is merely a scientific curiosity and no useful purpose has been found for it.''

''None at all?'' Samuel asked, astonished.

''Benjamin Franklin did roast a turkey using electricity. But most people looked upon that demonstration as merely a stunt. I have no turkey to roast, but I do want you to experience the effects of electricity first hand.''

Professor Day hooked wires to a battery. ''Stand in a circle around the table and join hands,'' he directed.

The boys hesitated.

Samuel Morse said, ''I'll do it!'' He took one of the wires.

Joseph Dulles stepped forward next. Soon a daisy

chain of linked students waited for the last student to take the wire and complete the circuit.

Samuel Barrell took the wire. In an instant the electric current shot around the chain of students. A howl of surprise echoed through the basement laboratory.

"Ouch!" Samuel Morse said. He threw down the wire. "It felt as though someone struck a light blow across my arms."

"Everyone felt the shock at the same time," Samuel wrote home to Sidney.

Later in the year, when Benjamin Silliman, who taught chemistry, touched on the subject, Samuel volunteered to help in the laboratory. Silliman let him take a battery apart and learn how it worked. The simplicity surprised him.

"A voltaic cell is nothing more than two plates of copper and zinc dipped in salt water," Samuel said. "Why has electricity remained merely a scientific curiosity?"

Benjamin Silliman explained, "Scientists are seldom good inventors. Instead, they pursue general laws of nature. It takes a person with a practical turn of mind to apply the discoveries to everyday inventions."

During the early morning of December 23, 1807, as Samuel walked to the chapel in the darkness before dawn, a remarkable sight appeared in the sky. The fiery trail of a shooting star streaked across the sky and burst with a loud explosion.

Students who'd been inside the chapel heard the sound, too, and hurried out to see what caused the noise.

"It's a meteor that fell to earth," Samuel said.

The shooting star was the topic of conversation during breakfast. Samuel set his tray of hashed meat, toast, and mug of hot chocolate on the table.

"Mr. Silliman saddled a horse and rode off to investigate," Samuel said as he sat down. "What do you think he will find?"

"Nothing," one of the boys answered promptly. He waved a fork in the air. "A meteor is something in the atmosphere, like lightning."

"No," Samuel said. "Not like lightning at all."

"You've been listening to Mr. Silliman too much," the boy said.

"What do you mean?"

"He thinks meteors are objects from out in space that wander into earth's path. Hah! Meteors are caused by nothing more than weather conditions."

That night Benjamin Silliman returned. He triumphantly held up a canvas bag heavy with samples. "I recovered several pieces of the object. It lay scattered around a number of miles." He opened the canvas bag and took out one of the blackened stones.

Samuel Morse studied the pitted surface. He picked it up. "It's much heavier than I expected."

"Watch this," Silliman said. He passed a magnet over one of the smaller stones. It leaped to the magnet and stuck with a dull clang.

"It's made of iron!" Samuel said.

"You're right," Silliman agreed.

"But how can iron rocks fall from the sky?"

"Not from the sky, but from the heavens—from the void between the planets." Benjamin Silliman smiled ruefully. "My view of the matter is not held by many others. I'll write a report about this and publish it for other scientists to consider."

"Will they believe you?"

"Perhaps. But scientists are cautious people. They are reluctant to accept a new idea."

Benjamin Silliman did publish his study of the meteor. Scientists greeted the report with an uproar of criticism, as he predicted.

He even received a letter from Thomas Jefferson. Silliman read the letter to Morse. ''The president is an amateur scientist. He writes, 'I find it easier to believe that a Yankee Professor would lie than that rocks would fall from the sky.' Jefferson doesn't mean it, of course, but he does express what many others think.''

Benjamin Silliman used a box-like device to help him make detailed drawings of the meteorites.

''What's this?'' Samuel asked. ''It looks like some sort of weapon.''

''It's a *camera obscura*,'' Benjamin Silliman said. ''A lens in the front throws an image on the frosted glass. Look for yourself.'' He turned the camera obscura so it pointed out the window.

Samuel Morse studied the image on the screen. The camera obscura faithfully reproduced the picket fence, red brick buildings, the courtyard, trees, and even students walking back and forth.

Benjamin Silliman said, ''A camera obscura is standard equipment for some artists. Scientists use it, too, to make exact drawings of rock formations, specimens collected in the field such as shells, and so on. I lay a thin sheet of paper on the glass and trace the image with a pencil.''

''It's too bad we can't capture the image,'' Samuel said.

''Hum . . . There may be a way.''

''What do you mean?''

''Certain chemicals react to light. Fetch the bottle of silver bromide crystals for me,'' Silliman directed.

Silliman dissolved the silver bromide crystals in water, then poured the solution into a tray and soaked a piece of paper in the solution. ''Let's replace the frosted glass with the paper and see if an image can be made.''

Samuel put the paper in the camera obscura and pointed the lens out the window to the brightly lighted courtyard. After fifteen minutes they inspected the paper. Nothing.

Silliman left the laboratory, but Samuel continued to experiment. He increased the exposure to an hour. Still nothing . . . no . . . a faint shadow appeared on the paper, the outline of the window.

"How is it going?" Silliman asked upon his return.

"Something's here—but it looks wrong somehow," Samuel said.

Silliman examined the paper. "The light and dark areas are reversed. The bright light of the window is black, but the dark shadows are white."

They left the paper on the table with the intention of working on the idea again the next day. But when Samuel saw the paper the next day, he cried out in dismay. "The paper has turned entirely black."

Silliman nodded thoughtfully. "The paper turned black because it was left in the light."

"What are we to do?" Samuel asked.

Silliman said, "Maybe we can think of a way to fix the image so it will not fade."

But Samuel soon forgot the photography experiments and moved on to other matters.

Samuel and his friends purchased a large amount of paper from a nearby paper mill. They pasted together a gigantic paper balloon eighteen feet high. The boys suspended it from a tower and lit a fire under the balloon to fill it with hot air.

The balloon soared aloft and vanished in the distance. The boys clamored off to recover their paper airship.

"It needs repairs," Barrell said.

"We'll fix it as good as new," Samuel said.

They patched it and prepared to raise the balloon

again. In their second attempt, a sudden gust of wind caused the fire to blaze up. The paper took fire. The balloon soared in flames and fell back to earth in ashes.

"It was a glorious sight while it lasted," Samuel wrote home.

In his letters home, Samuel took care to thank his parents for the sacrifices they made to keep him in school. By his senior year at Yale all three of the Morse children were there—Samuel in the senior class, Sidney in the junior class, and Richard in the sophomore class. The expenses were almost more than Jedediah Morse could handle.

Two months before graduation, Samuel Morse still had not told his father that he wanted to be a painter.

He did reveal his plans to Jannette Hart of Saybrook. He'd painted a miniature portrait of her, and become fascinated by her beauty. She had fine features, a beautiful complexion, rich brown hair, and large eyes.

She thought Samuel Morse was wonderful, too. "Your father knows all of the right people," she gushed.

Samuel and Jannette often went for long walks together. He told her about his burning ambition to be a painter.

"Washington Allston, one of the greatest American painters, is in Boston now. Mr. Allston saw one of my miniatures. He said I show promise."

Jannette Hart's pretty face puckered into a frown. "But painters are vagabonds. They're not welcome in polite company."

"Good artists are welcomed in the best homes. John Copley lives in a beautiful home on Beacon Hill. Look at Gilbert Stuart and his portraits of famous Americans. Look at Benjamin West. He's president of the Royal Academy in England."

Jannette asked, ''Have you told your parents you want to be an artist?''

''No . . .'' Samuel said slowly. ''I've not yet worked up the courage.''

Finally, Samuel composed a letter to his father. ''I think that I was made for a painter. I should desire to study with Mr. Washington Allston during the winter. He expects to return to England in the spring, and I should like to go with him.''

His father's answer was short and to the point. ''Your mama and I have been thinking and planning for you. I shall disclose to you our plan when I see you. Until then suspend your mind.''

After graduation Samuel Morse learned their plans. He told Jannette Hart the news.

''I'm to be an apprentice printer and bookseller in the shop of Daniel Mallory in Boston.''

She murmured sympathetic words. But her eyes seemed pleased at the turn of events.

Samuel tried to put on a brave show. But alone in his room he packed his sketches. Dejected, he sat on the edge of his bed. He was so low in spirits he could almost cry.

3
A Yankee in London

Compared to the excitement and freedom of Yale, the bookstore job on Scolly Square was a bleak existence. Samuel worked from nine to twelve and from three to sunset. He spent long hours bent over a desk, writing purchase orders and keeping account books.

On the way home, however, he often walked to Court Street to visit Washington Allston's studio. The painter welcomed Samuel warmly and gave him encouragement.

"How is the young painter doing?"

"All right, I suppose," Morse said without enthusiasm.

Washington Allston asked, "Have you heard about Dr. Warren's lectures in anatomy? He knows the human body as well as any man in the United States."

"I want to be an artist, not a doctor."

"My friend, an artist must know the muscles and bones of the body to draw it correctly. I suggest you attend his lectures."

Samuel brightened. "When does he speak?"

"Every day at one o'clock," Allston told him. "You can go during your noon break from work."

"I'll attend!" Samuel promised.

A few days later, Samuel came bouncing into the studio. His face was aglow with excitement.

"The lectures are extremely interesting," Samuel said.

"Are you painting again?"

"Yes. I've outfitted a studio in a room over the kitchen at home. I have a fire there and I can spend my time working alone at night."

"But the light, Samuel. Painting at night without natural light is difficult."

"I've bought one of the new lamps with a glass chimney. It cost six dollars and gives excellent light."

"Have you finished a painting?"

"Only one," Morse said. He unrolled the drawing. "It's a family portrait for Nancy Shepherd, my nurse. I want your opinion before I give it to her."

The painting showed the Morse family gathered around a table in Jedediah's study. Sitting at one end of the table was Elizabeth, his mother, with a white mobcap on her head and a knitting basket at her feet. The house cat, looking smug and contented, sat on the patterned rug. Samuel and his brothers stood around the table. They watched as Jedediah explained a feature on the globe in the middle of the table.

Samuel said, "Richard, the boy in the rumpled clothes, is youngest. He's decided to study theology and become a minister. Sidney has the ruffled hair and solemn expression. He's going to be a lawyer."

Washington Allston pinned the drawing down and stepped back to look at it.

"What do you think?" Samuel asked.

"The colors are good; the features detailed,"

Washington Allston said. ''But the composition is stiff and the figures awkward.''

Washington saw Samuel's hurt expression and clamped a hand on Samuel's shoulder. ''But it's very good considering you've had no formal training. You'll improve.''

''But how shall I improve without proper training?''

''I've talked with your father,'' Washington Allston said. ''He's agreed to a test.''

''A test?''

Allston explained, ''Next year before I leave for England, an expert painter will judge your work. If he sees talent, then your father will let you go with me to study in London.''

Samuel Morse threw himself into his painting. He finished a landscape and a historical canvas titled *Landing of the Pilgrims*. Washington Allston pronounced the paintings first rate.

At last the unveiling came. Jedediah arrived at the Allston studio with the artist to judge the paintings. In walked the man famous for his portraits of George Washington—Gilbert Stuart.

Slowly the great man took in every detail of the landscape. He turned from it in dismissal. Clearly the painting did not impress him. Next he examined the canvas showing the Pilgrims landing at Plymouth.

Samuel held his breath.

Gilbert Stuart frowned at the pilgrim with the feather in a tricornered hat. He winced when he saw the man's legs cut off at the knees by the picture frame. He shook his head at the distorted landing boat.

The tension in the studio grew.

Gilbert Stuart peered closely at the background. He noted the richly textured hills and rolling clouds, and the lifelike colors in the faces.

''Well managed,'' Gilbert Stuart said at last. ''Dr.

Morse, your son has my approval.''

Samuel Morse could hardly contain his pleasure. ''To England then,'' he said with satisfaction.

''You'll be away from home for three years,'' Washington Allston said. ''Say your goodbyes.''

Samuel Morse grew thoughtful. ''Yes, I must see Jannette before I leave.''

When Samuel saw Jannette, he described in vivid details the minutes of silence while Stuart inspected the paintings. ''I thought my lungs would burst.''

''So you're going to London?'' she asked in a flat voice.

''Yes, isn't it great? When I come back I'll be an accomplished painter. And then we . . .'' He hesitated. ''Jannette, if you will wait upon my training we can be married when I return.''

Her pretty face wrinkled into angry lines. She stamped her foot. ''Never! You can't go tramping off to England and expect me to wait for you. When you come back what will you be? Nothing but a common portrait painter. Listen to me, Samuel Morse . . . No. I have nothing more to say! Goodbye!'' She slammed the door in his face.

Samuel, stunned at her outburst, waited for a moment at the gate. Slowly he turned and walked away.

You rush from one foolish whim to another, his father had said. Not anymore. He'd let nothing divert him from painting. Someday his paintings would be known throughout America—throughout the world!

Samuel Morse took passage on the ship *Lydia* with Mr. Allston and a dozen other passengers. The voyage began from new York harbor on July 13, 1811. The ship's sails caught good winds and crossed the Atlantic in the nearly record time of twenty-two days.

Samuel, who'd always wanted to travel, enjoyed the trip immensely. At Liverpool, he stepped from the ship tanned and happy. ''I see no reason why people should dread a sea voyage,'' he said to Washington Allston.

Washington Allston had sailed the Atlantic before. ''We had good weather, fair winds, and pleasant companions. But sea voyages are not always so enjoyable,'' he warned. ''Our return voyage may be made under the clouds of war.''

Hundreds of people stood at the docks. They listened eagerly for word from the United States. ''Is it war?'' someone called.

''No,'' Washington Allston answered. ''But war will surely come if something isn't done.''

Because of England's war with Napoleon in France, the British government passed an order which allowed British ships to interfere with American sailing. Acting under these Orders of Council, British vessels captured

American ships en route to France. They swooped
down and pressed American sailors into service on
British warships.

Samuel Morse landed in England at a time when
tensions between the United States and England grew
more strained by the day.

The mayor of Liverpool summoned Samuel and
Allston. "You have only ten days to reach London
or you'll be put under arrest," Mayor Drinkwater
said. He thrust the travel documents into their hands.

Samuel and Allston hired a wagon to haul their
belongings to London. "What a chilly welcome!"
Samuel said. "We've done nothing to offend
England."

"Oh, but we have," Allston said. "Our country
has refused to trade with England. Look at the goods
piled up and unsold on the docks. The economy of
England suffers terribly. Factories are closed and
hungry workers are marching in the streets."

Samuel looked around the docks. Crates, barrels,
and bales of goods stood piled to dizzy heights.
Hungry-eyed dockhands waited listlessly for work to
come their way. "All of this could be avoided,"
Samuel predicted, "by repealing the Orders of
Council."

"Maybe they will be repealed. The Orders of
Council are almost as unpopular here as in America."

Samuel found temporary lodging in London at 67
Great Titchfield Street. He immediately wrote to his
parents announcing his arrival. In his first letter home,
Samuel expressed a wish that, at the time, seemed to
be nothing more than a fanciful idea.

"I only wish," he wrote, "you had this letter now
to relieve your minds from anxiety. I can imagine
Mother wishing that she could hear of my arrival and
thinking of the thousands of accidents which may have
befallen me."

Samuel paused a moment and sharpened the quill. Thoughtfully, he added, "I wish in an instant I could communicate the information. But three thousand miles are not passed over in an instant. We must wait four long weeks before we can hear from each other."

London, home of the British empire, sprawled along the Thames. After the great fire of 1666, Sir Christopher Wren directed its rebuilding. He made it into a modern city with tall churches, elegant homes, and noble government buildings.

Samuel walked to Somerset House. He easily identified it by the bust of Michelangelo over the entrance. It was the home of the Royal Academy.

Samuel took a deep breath before knocking on the door. Clutching the letter of introduction from his father, he wondered what to expect of Benjamin West. The great painter had been born of poor Quaker parents in the backwoods of Pennsylvania. As a child, West made his own brushes and learned from the Indians to mix colors using wild plants and juice of berries. Now, in his old age, he held the most powerful post in the art world, president of the Royal Academy of London.

A bright-eyed gentleman opened the door.

"Yes? Speak, young man."

"I . . . I wish to see Benjamin West," Samuel stammered.

"Yes, yes, come in my young friend. Mr. Allston told me to expect you. Come on. Follow me." The man rushed ahead, scrambling up the long flight of marble stairs.

Morse quickened his steps. "Is Mr. West here?"

"I'm West," the man said. "Come along. I've a secret I want to show you."

The legendary Benjamin West! Why, he was seventy-five years old! Yet, this man scrambled up the stairs and strode down the hall like a man years younger.

Samuel puffed along behind. He glanced quickly to either side. West's sketches hung from floor to ceiling all along the gallery.

They walked into the studio. West threw back a sheet of wrapping paper hanging along one wall.

"Here's something I've not shown anyone else," West said. "I'm working on the sketches for my next painting. You're the first to see it."

Samuel drew in his breath, surprised at the size of the drawing. "Why, the finished painting will be enormous."

"Gilbert Stuart calls them 'ten acre paintings.' This one shows Christ before Pilate and will contain about fifty or sixty life-size figures."

"I'm looking forward to working with you at the Royal Academy," Samuel said. "I can hardly wait to begin."

"Ah, you sound so eager. Listen to me, my young American friend, you've got to earn a place in the Royal Academy. Many British students want to attend, so in these troubled times I can't be accused of playing favorites by selecting my countrymen. Bring me a drawing worthy of entrance."

"What subject would be best?" Samuel asked.

Benjamin West brushed aside clutter from a table and selected a small Greek statue. "Reproduce this on paper," he said.

Samuel accepted the statue. "I'll render it to my best ability."

Suddenly Benjamin West grabbed Samuel's hands. "Put the statue down. Let me tie you with this cord."

"What?"

"Sit still a moment. I want to sketch your hands."

"For what purpose?" Samuel asked, baffled.

"For my painting. I've been looking for the hands of Christ. You'll be the model."

Samuel held his hands as Benjamin West directed.

The old gentleman talked as he worked, touching on a dozen different subjects. "Noble paintings, I believe, call for noble subjects chosen from great events of history, or from the Bible, or from great literature."

At last he finished the sketch. With a twinkle in his eyes, Benjamin West said, "When my painting is complete you may say you had a *hand* in it."

Samuel found himself under test again. This time he had to produce a drawing worthy of entry into the Royal Academy.

Benjamin West agreed to review the drawing. Samuel spent two weeks in drawing a charcoal sketch of the statue. Finally he dared to present it to Benjamin West.

"Admirable," West said. "Very well, my young friend, go on and finish it."

"It is finished," Samuel said.

"Oh, no," said Mr. West. "Look here and here and here." He pointed to the areas lost in shadow and to a hand that looked like a mitten.

"Yes . . . I see it now," Samuel admitted. "I'll touch it up and have it back right away."

A week passed. Samuel struggled to eliminate even the smallest imperfection. Again he presented the drawing to the sharp eyes of West.

"Well done, indeed. Go on and finish it."

"Isn't it finished?" Morse asked.

"Not yet," West replied. "See, you have not marked the muscles nor the fingers." He handed it back to Samuel. "It is not numerous drawings, but the character of one drawing which makes a painter."

Samuel diligently spent another three days retouching his drawing. But—

"Very clever, indeed," West said. "Go on and finish it."

"I cannot finish it," Morse said. Despair filled his voice.

"Well," West said. "I have tried you long enough. You have learned to finish one picture, and that is what makes a painter. Welcome to the Royal Academy!"

Humbly, Samuel admitted, "I have learned more by drawing this one picture than I would have accomplished in twice the time by a dozen half-finished sketches."

Samuel spent most of his time at the Royal Academy. He studied paintings by the old masters and tried to duplicate their colors, textures, and compositions. He avoided his room whenever possible.

"My room is so dreary and lonely," Samuel explained to Washington Allston.

"You took the room as temporary quarters," Allston pointed out. "Now is the time to move to a larger apartment."

"I haven't the money for anything better," Samuel said.

"Then share an apartment," Allston suggested. "I know a young artist who's looking for a roommate. Let me take you to him."

Washington Allston introduced Samuel Morse and Charles R. Leslie.

"I'll find a place for us," Leslie volunteered. "I was born in London."

"Oh?" Samuel said, his enthusiasm growing cold immediately. "I thought you were an American."

"Set your mind at ease," Leslie said. "My parents were living in London when I was born, but I'm an American, educated in Philadelphia."

The two young men agreed to take an apartment together.

As promised, Charles Leslie found an apartment. "It's Number 4 Buckingham Place, Fitzroy Square. Robert Fulton lived here at one time," Leslie said.

"Robert Fulton, the inventor?"

"Yes, the same man, but Fulton came to London to study to be an artist. He grew interested in engineering and went on to invent the steamboat."

"Why would anyone give up an artistic career to become an inventor?" Samuel wondered.

"He certainly knew how to choose an apartment. It has two good windows. I'll set my easel in front on one and you can have the other."

"Let's paint portraits of each other," Morse said.

"In these clothes?" Leslie asked. "There's no color. The portraits will be too somber."

The next day Samuel came into the room with two packages. "Come here, Leslie." he said, "I've rented costumes to wear for our portraits."

Samuel cut the string and opened the package. "My

clothing is a Scottish highland outfit, complete with a feathered headdress and tartan plaid skirt. For you I have a fancy Spanish suit and cloak.''

The first portraits they painted in London were of each other. In their room they painted the hours away, sometimes talking, sometimes deep in thought as one or the other struggled to force color and life into the canvas. In all the time they worked together, Samuel Morse and Charles Leslie never had a falling out.

But in the world outside their windows, things were not going as well. Tension between the United States and Britain had reached the breaking point. Either the hateful Orders of Council would have to be repealed, or America would declare war.

4

Canvas and Cannons

Washington Allston often visited the two young art students. He came as both friend and teacher.

"Good news," Washington Allston said one day as he stepped into their apartment. "There will be no war."

Samuel wiped off his brush. "Why?"

"The Orders of Council have been repealed!"

But it came too late. Only two days after England struck down the orders, the United States declared war.

"The message didn't get to America in time," Washington Allston said glumly. "Battles were being fought while ships set sail to carry the news to President Madison."

"What will it mean for us? Should we go home?" Samuel asked.

"I think not," Allston said. "The shipping lanes between England and America have been closed and we're pretty much stranded here. We'll have to make the best of it. Continue with your studies. I'll call upon you daily until we learn the mood of the people.''

After a few weeks the two boys learned they would be tolerated as long as they went about their studies.

The time came for Samuel Morse to paint his first professional painting. The canvas would be entered in a contest sponsored each year by the Royal Academy.

Benjamin West asked, ''Have you chosen your subject?''

''Not yet, except it will be a small painting.''

''Why small?'' West asked.

''I've been told that small paintings have better chances of being accepted. A place to hang one is more easily found in the exhibition.''

Benjamin West disagreed. ''Paint as large as possible,'' he urged.

Reluctantly, Samuel agreed to follow West's advice. He measured a canvas eight feet by six feet and set to work. He chose as his subject the *Dying Hercules*.

After two weeks, Washington Allston came to give his opinion of the work.

Samuel said, ''You're a friend, and not given to empty flattery. Tell me the truth about the painting.''

Washington Allston didn't mince words. ''Very bad. That is not flesh. It is mud. It is painted with brick dust and clay.''

''What am I going to do?'' Samuel cried. He gripped the palette knife, ready to thrust it through the canvas in frustration.

''Have you made a model?'' Washington Allston asked.

''I'm a painter, not a sculptor,'' Samuel said.

''Ah, but the old masters often made models first.''

Samuel took Allston's advice. He modeled the figure in clay. Both Allston and West praised the statue.

Allston said, ''This is better than anything you have done. Have plaster casts made of it. Send one home to your parents so they can see your work.''

Benjamin West said, ''And enter the model in the Adelphi Society of Arts competition.''

Samuel entered the *Dying Hercules* in the sculpture competition. He went back to the painting and used the statue as a guide. This time he made much better progress.

Before Samuel finished the painting, Washington Allston called him to the Adelphi Society for the awards program. Samuel dressed in his best clothes. Even so, he felt out of place among the gentlemen wearing long waistcoats, dress swords, and cocked hats with feather plumes. The high-born ladies wore fancy dresses of silk and satin.

''What am I doing here?'' Samuel asked.

Washington Allston said, ''Your statue of Hercules may have won an award.''

''Unlikely,'' Samuel said. ''The British would hardly give an American an award in times like these.''

As they watched the proceedings, Washington Allston pointed out Lord Percy, as well as ambassadors from foreign countries.

The proceedings drew to a close. The Duke of Norfolk stepped to the podium to give the final award, a gold medal. ''For the best sculpture, first prize to Mr. Samuel Finley Breese Morse for his statue in plaster of the *Dying Hercules*.''

Not only had the clay model won first place and a gold medal, but after he finished his painting it was singled out as one of the dozen best paintings at the Royal Academy exhibit. Because of its large size, the painting dominated the gallery wall at Somerset House. In the painting, Samuel captured the pain in the twisted body of Hercules as he made his final, noble struggle.

Samuel could write home with a certain amount of pride.

"Six hundred pictures were refused admission this year," Samuel wrote. "Of the two thousand at the exhibition, the newspapers put my *Dying Hercules* in the top twelve.

"Something about the *Dying Hercules* caught the imagination of the people of England. It has been well received. Perhaps it takes more courage to face defeat than to win a victory.

"I hear various preachers on Sundays. Sometimes it is Mr. Burke, but most commonly the Church of England clergy because there's a church in my neighborhood. Mr. Burke's congregation is three miles distant."

He folded the paper, melted wax with a candle and sealed the letter. He pressed his ring into the wax. As a postscript he added, "The seal of the letter is worth noticing. It's the one Michelangelo used. My ring is an impression from the original."

Samuel carefully packed the painting and the little statue of the *Dying Hercules*. He sent the package to Liverpool to be shipped home to his parents.

As the War of 1812 dragged on, mail between America and England became impossibly slow. Letters ran fifteen months late. Samuel asked about his painting of Hercules and the plaster cast of the statue. Two years passed and he heard nothing from his mother concerning the shipment.

In 1814 the war with the United States ended in the same way it had begun, amid confusion caused by poor communication. The Battle of new Orleans was fought eleven days *after* the signing of the peace treaty.

Now Samuel began receiving letters from home. "The painting of the *Dying Hercules* has at last been received," his mother wrote. "But the plaster cast is still missing."

Although England's war with the United States ended, the conflict against Napoleon grew more intense. The outcome was in doubt. In May of 1815, London was rife with rumors that the war with Napoleon had reached its final stages. In London, the city leaders arranged for the cannons in Hyde Park to fire as a signal of victory. But the cannons remained silent.

One evening in June of 1815, as Samuel Morse attended a party, he wandered into a room to be alone. As he sat before an open window, he heard the distant boom of the Hyde Park cannons.

He rushed to tell his host. Soon the entire party gathered by the window. In the stillness, the rumble of the guns sounded again.

"Victory! Napoleon is defeated! Peace at last!" the guests cried.

The British had finally defeated Napoleon at the Battle of Flanders, in a place called Waterloo. A few days later the Treaty of Paris was signed.

Samuel made his plans to return home. But could he earn a living as an artist?

"It seems more difficult than I first supposed," Samuel confided to Allston. "Leslie took ten months to paint his picture, and my Hercules cost me nearly a year's study."

Allston agreed. "Large pictures are not the work of a moment. But the rewards can be enormous. Look at West. He doesn't sell his painting once, but many times over."

"How do you mean?" Samuel asked.

"Take his painting of Christ healing the sick. First

he put it on display, and the public paid an admission to see the picture. Then West sold engravings of the painting as souvenirs. Finally, he auctioned off the painting itself. The one painting earned a small fortune.''

Samuel shook his head, ''It seems unbecoming for a great man like West to be so commercial.''

''You'll learn, my young friend,'' Allston said, ''that an artist must scratch for money.''

Because of the war, Samuel had spent an extra year in England. Four years to the day after he landed in Liverpool, Samuel arrived in that city again, this time to arrange passage home.

''Which ship sails first?'' Samuel asked the ticket agent.

''The *Ceres*,'' the man said.

Samuel visited the ship. He came back, not clearly decided. The captain seemed to be a surly man, abrupt and uninterested in showing him around.

''The accommodations are not first rate,'' Samuel said.

''Wait for another ship,'' the agent said. ''It matters not to me.''

Samuel drummed his fingers on the table. He didn't want to wait. ''I'll take it,'' he said at last.

On August 21, 1815, Samuel boarded the *Ceres*, looking forward to a pleasant voyage. Instead, the trip home turned out to be a long and dreadful one.

For fourteen days the vessel waited in Liverpool harbor, becalmed. Finally at three o'clock one afternoon they sailed, along with two hundred other ships that had been waiting for favorable winds.

By morning the ships had scattered to their separate ways. From the deck of the *Ceres* Samuel couldn't see another ship. Instead, thick gray clouds dominated the sky.

The ship sailed into the gale, fighting the contrary

winds. Rain lashed at the rigging, and waves crashed on the deck. The passengers stayed below and suffered the agony of sea sickness.

At the end of ten days, they'd covered only three hundred miles.

Samuel tried to forget the storm by going over his plans for the future. He'd written ahead encouraging his parents to ask around for people who wanted portraits made. In his baggage he'd packed a roll of unpainted canvas, enough for a great canvas and at least fifty full-size portraits.

In addition, he'd painted a colossal painting called *The Judgment of Jupiter*. He would display it at his studio in Boston and charge admission to those who viewed it.

Samuel took a letter from his pocket. He'd carried it since receiving it from his brother Sidney. He unfolded the well-worn letter and read the paragraph about Jannette Hart again.

"Jannette has married a rich, middle-aged merchant," Sidney wrote. "She dresses in regal clothing and is the center of society. She seems quite happy."

After three weeks, when the wind died down, Samuel walked on deck. His knees were wobbly from the days of confinement below deck.

In the distance to the south he saw a large ship, its masts ripped off. A puff of smoke came from a small cannon on the bow of the crippled ship. A few seconds later he heard the bark of the explosion.

"Why is the ship firing the gun?" Samuel asked.

"It's a signal of distress," a deck hand said.

Samuel waited for the captain to change direction and go to the ship's aid.

The other passengers gathered at the rail. They pointed at the derelict, clearly visible now, with distress flags flying.

"Why do we ignore them?" Samuel asked. "It

must be terrible for them to see help, but for us to sail away.''

The deck hand shrugged. ''Ask the captain.''

The passengers went to the captain and demanded he change course.

''I'm the master of this ship,'' the captain said, ''and we've lost too much time already. Two other ships have been sighted. They can help.'' The captain turned to leave.

Samuel grabbed his arm. ''But we're the nearest,'' Samuel said. ''We must rescue them.''

The captain shook Samuel's hand away. In an overbearing, pompous voice he said, ''I am the master here. I give the orders.''

''You're the master at sea, but not on shore. I assure you,'' Samuel warned, ''if you fail to set course to rescue them, I will expose your lack of humanity as soon as we land in Boston. The owners of this ship will take you to account.''

With a sour look the captain motioned to the first mate. They talked together in whispers. At last the ship changed course, but at reduced speed.

By nightfall the ship received aid, but from the two other ships. It became clear the captain of the *Ceres* had intentionally delayed to avoid the trouble of helping the wreck.

''We could have been there by noon,'' Samuel said.

The next morning, Samuel awoke to an incredible sight. The sea looked like a mirror, not a ripple on its surface. ''It looks as if we are at anchor in a harbor,'' Samuel said to another passenger.

''But look at the dark clouds in the southwest,'' the passenger pointed out.

''Bad weather again,'' Samuel agreed.

''Worse weather if I'm any judge. The storm we're heading for will make the gale of a few days ago seem like a gentle breeze.''

The storm struck. The captain ordered all of the sails taken in. The wind roared through the bare rigging. Waves like gray mountains broke over the deck. The ship rolled so badly Samuel and the other passengers kept to their berths, strapped in to prevent falling to the floor.

Samuel cried, ''Oh! Who would go to sea when he can stay on shore!''

The little *Ceres* fell victim to alternate gales and calms. Passengers and crew nearly gave up hope of reaching land. Food supplies fell dangerously low. They ran out of beans, and what little bread remained turned moldy.

With gloomy apprehension, they learned that the captain spent hours pouring over the charts, trying to learn their position.

On the fifty-eighth day, as darkness came upon them, the lookout cried, ''Land!''

The passengers ran to the rail. ''Where are we?'' Morse asked.

''The land is Cape Cod!''

After midnight, the ship made landfall—Boston and home!

5

Tramp Painter

The parsonage on Main Street just below Breed's Hill seemed the same, as if nothing had changed. Nancy Shepherd still ran the kitchen. Prince still faithfully pulled the chaise carrying Dr. Jedediah Morse to visit his congregation. Even Samuel felt like a small boy again as his mother engulfed him in her arms.

"Richard's not home this weekend, but he'll be back next week. He's studying in Andover for the ministry," Mrs. Morse said.

"And Sidney?" Samuel asked.

Jedediah Morse spoke, "He has launched the weekly *Recorder* in Boston."

"A newspaper?" Samuel asked.

"A religious paper," Jedediah said. "It is one of the first religious journals in the country."

After unpacking, Samuel asked about his statue of the *Dying Hercules*.

"We have the painting," his mother said, "but the statue never came."

"I still have the mold," Samuel said. "I'll cast additional copies."

Jedediah Morse said, "I've rented a studio for you in Boston. It's on Cornhill Square, near Mallory's bookstore where you used to work."

In the two small rooms of the brick building, Samuel opened his studio. He exhibited the *Dying Hercules* and the *Judgment of Jupiter*.

Sidney printed an announcement in the *Recorder* to invite the public:

Morse's
Exhibition of Pictures
Joy's building, Cornhill Square

Hundreds of people made it a point to meet the young artist, Benjamin West's best-known student. They admired his paintings with oh's and ah's and invited Samuel to their teas and parties. Samuel set up his easel, ready for the orders to come his way.

But not a single person offered to purchase the paintings. Despite social recognition, no commissions and no customers came his way.

A year passed. During that time, Samuel received not a single order for a historical canvas. He spent his time making portraits of relatives and friends. Samuel gave up one of the rooms of his studio, and then the other.

Samuel tried to figure out why he failed to sell his paintings. "Portrait painting alone is profitable in this country," he decided. "But in Boston, Gilbert Stuart is the master of portrait painting. I can't compete with him."

"What do you propose to do?" Sidney asked.

"Gilbert Stuart seldom goes into the towns and villages," Samuel said. "I'll travel into the rural areas, away from Boston and other large cities."

"But they hardly know you elsewhere," Sidney pointed out.

"Father's name is known everywhere. I'll ask him to write letters of introduction," Samuel said. "If customers will not come to my studio, I must take my studio to them."

He packed for the tour—paints, brushes, samples of portraits, canvas, and millboard for less expensive portraits.

How much should he charge? Samuel didn't know. Gilbert Stuart charged a hundred dollars or so for each portrait. At first, Samuel offered the portraits at fifty dollars each. But he quickly learned the country people could not afford that price. For his rustic customers, he reduced the price even lower.

In Concord, New Hampshire, Samuel sought out Reverend Asa McFarland at his church. Samuel needed somewhere to stay while in Concord.

"By all means, lodge with me," Reverend McFarland said.

They walked along the wide, dusty main street to the minister's old-fashioned, square home shaded by elms and maples.

"What do you charge for your paintings?" Reverend McFarland asked.

"Fifteen dollars," Samuel said. "Six years ago, before being trained by Benjamin West, I painted miniatures at Yale for five dollars."

"Well, you should offer to paint Lucretia Walker for free. She's the most beautiful girl in all of New England."

Samuel knew that ministers considered it their duty to be matchmakers. Even so, he'd already heard about Miss Walker, the pride of Concord.

"I've met enough charming girls who find a tramp painter below their dignity," Samuel said ruefully. "I'd prefer to let some other deserving bachelor make her acquaintance."

Within two weeks, Samuel painted five portraits. A customer named Samuel Sparhawk invited him to a dinner party at his home.

The night of the party, Samuel stepped onto the porch of the Sparhawk home. As he knocked at the door, he heard the voice of a young woman speaking inside the house. ''I have always wanted to meet the famous Samuel Morse,'' she said. ''His paintings elevate the mind.''

Samuel strode into the room, anxious to meet someone with such sound judgment.

Sparhawk introduced Samuel to the girl. She was seventeen years old, slight, dark haired, lively, and well educated. Her name? ''Miss Lucretia Pickering Walker,'' Sparhawk said.

Miss Walker instantly cast her spell upon Samuel. He found excuses to prolong his stay in Concord to be with her.

Samuel wrote home, ''I am still in Concord and passing my time very agreeably.'' He didn't explain to his mother or father why his stay had become so enjoyable.

But to Leslie, in London, he wrote a long letter describing the beautiful Lucretia Walker. ''She is a young lady of great personal loveliness and rare good sense. Yet modest, quiet, frank, and kindhearted.''

Leslie could not resist poking fun at his friend. ''You have described her in such delicious terms your pen should flow with honey instead of ink!''

Finally, when he could delay his departure from Concord no longer, Samuel told Lucretia his heart.

''Love and painting are quarrelsome companions,'' Samuel admitted. ''But I've been unable to turn away from love. Before I go, I must know if you feel the same.''

She said, ''My heart is like yours. I love you, too, Samuel.''

But marriage was out of the question. ''I haven't earned enough money yet,'' Samuel said.

With renewed vigor he set out again, tramping through the rural towns of New Hampshire and Vermont. He earned enough to support himself, but not enough to support a wife.

Lucretia stood by him during the trying days. ''You'll be successful someday,'' she said.

Someday, but not soon enough.

He went home for the winter.

His mother said, ''My brother has written from Charleston, South Carolina. He's invited you to open a studio there.''

Samuel shook his head. South Carolina was a thousand miles from his beloved Lucretia.

Samuel read the letter. ''The people of South Carolina,'' Dr. James Finley wrote, ''appreciate the finer things of life. Portrait commissions can be found among the many rich planters and merchants in Charleston.''

Samuel visited Lucretia. ''My uncle thinks I'll earn more in a few months in the South than I would in several years in New England.''

Lucretia said, ''By all means go, if it will mean we can marry sooner.''

In January of 1818, Samuel Morse sailed for Charleston, the capital of South Carolina. In that beautiful city he enjoyed an early spring, with mild climate and the gracious warmth of Southern hospitality.

Dr. James Finley cordially welcomed Samuel and introduced him to his friends—planters, lawyers, and merchants.

Samuel settled at Uncle Finley's house on King Street. During the first month, he was swept up in a round of activities—hunting, riding, fishing, sailing, and lawn parties.

Surrounded by such wealth, Samuel felt the prospects to be good. He rented a studio room over Aubin's store. It was a favorable location, down a narrow street with vine-covered garden walls on both sides.

But no sitters came.

Samuel grew weary of inactivity and being away from Lucretia. Finally, he made the decision to go back home. He wrote to Lucretia, "Dearest Lucrece, my bad luck will be our good luck. I'm coming back to New England and to you."

But first, Samuel decided to pay for his Uncle Finley's hospitality by painting the doctor's portrait.

When the good citizens of Charleston saw the finished painting they were amazed. Samuel had accurately captured the likeness of Doctor Finley.

Colonel John Ashe Alston pronounced the painting first rate. "I have paintings by Benjamin West. Your portrait of Dr. Finley is worth two hundred dollars."

The incredible skill of Samuel Morse became the talk of the town. Planters, merchants, judges, clergymen, and generals came for portraits. In a few weeks more than one hundred fifty people asked for their portraits. The price? Sixty dollars each!

Samuel wrote Lucretia again. "My good luck is our bad luck. It will probably be late summer before I can come north to be married."

In only three months, Samuel finished fifty-three portraits. He worked sixteen hours a day. Still the sitters came. Samuel raised his rate to eighty dollars a portrait.

"I'll need a year's time to fulfill the present orders," Samuel told his Uncle Finley.

"But you want to go back north to marry Lucretia?"

"Yes," Samuel said. "What am I going to do? The work is here, but my heart is in New England."

Dr. Finley said, "You can come back next winter, or take the work with you."

"Take it with me?" Samuel asked. "Why, maybe I can. I'll make pencil sketches of my sitters. Later, during the summer in New England I can finish the paintings."

Samuel sailed home. After landing in Boston, he rode to Concord for a reunion with Lucretia.

"Dear Samuel," Lucretia said. "You must ask my parents for their blessings upon our marriage."

"I've proven that I can earn a reasonable income in portraiture. Now, if only I can convince your father."

While in London, Boston and Charleston, Samuel had spoken to men of power and wealth. But words failed him now. He couldn't bring himself to speak directly to Lucretia's father. Instead, he wrote a letter. He assured the Walkers of his love for their daughter. "I can provide for her," he wrote.

Samuel rode back to Boston and waited for their reply. Two weeks passed.

Finally, a letter arrived from Lucretia. With anxious hands, Samuel tore it open.

"Yes, Father and Mother have agreed to our marriage," she assured him.

Samuel expressed his joy. "Everything successful! Praise be to the Giver of every good gift!"

On the morning of September 29, 1818, Reverend Asa McFarland married Samuel Finley Breese Morse and Lucretia Pickering Walker in the Walker home.

Lucretia read about their wedding in the *Patriot*, the New Hampshire newspaper. "Look at this, Samuel," she said. She handed him the paper, folded to the place. "They call you the 'celebrated' painter."

Samuel smiled, "I'm much happier being called the 'employed' painter."

The honeymoon couple packed for South Carolina.

Samuel said, ''I've asked around for the best accommodations and arranged passage on the schooner *Tontine* to South Carolina. It is the best ship and has the best captain in the trade.''

The young couple spent the winter in Charleston. They settled in Mrs. Muro's boarding house on Church Street.

Lucretia was alarmed at the price of the room. ''Ten dollars a week!'' she exclaimed, aghast.

''Prices are higher here,'' Samuel said. ''You'll have to learn to adjust to the city.''

Lucretia did learn to adjust. She bloomed like the magnolias, her charm taking the city. The couple could not have been more happy.

''Several other artists have come to town while you were away,'' Dr. Finley told them. ''Your success has lured them to the city.''

''There's enough business to go around,'' Samuel said. ''My patrons are loyal. I have already as much work as I can accomplish.''

One day he was called to the home of Colonel John Alston. ''Let me speak frankly with you,'' Colonel Alston said. ''I'm annoyed by the fact that I've paid other artists more than two thousand dollars for family pictures and not one is a tolerable likeness. Will you paint my daughter, Sally, to your best ability?''

''My schedule is filled . . . ,'' Samuel began.

''I'll pay two hundred dollars.''

''But as a favor to you,'' Samuel continued hastily, ''I'll find time to paint little Sally.''

After he finished the painting, Colonel Alston paid the agreed-upon two hundred dollars. Samuel described the transaction to Lucretia. ''He wants me to make another painting next year—for four hundred dollars!''

''What a strange man,'' Lucretia said.

"I wish more of the rich people in this country would be as strange," Samuel said.

There was a knock on the door.

The man at the door carried an official-looking document. "My name is William Roach," the man said. "As you may know, President James Monroe will visit the city of Charleston."

"Yes," Samuel said. "He's the first president to tour the country since George Washington."

"The city council considers his visit an important historical event," Mr. Roach explained. "The council authorized me to ask you to make a portrait of the president."

Samuel read the city council resolution. They offered him seven hundred and fifty dollars for the portrait!

"Do you agree to the terms?" Mr. Roach asked.

"Certainly," Samuel said. "But will President Monroe sit for a picture?"

President Monroe arrived in the city with a rousing fireworks display. The president did agree to the painting, but, "It is impossible to discover time in my schedule for the sittings at present. Can you come to Washington?"

"Yes," Samuel quickly agreed.

"Very good, Mr. Morse," the president said. He promised to arrange a room for Samuel in the White House.

At the end of the season, Samuel and Lucretia went north again. They decided to settle in New Haven, Connecticut. Samuel had fond memories of the city from his time at Yale.

His neighbors included Benjamin Silliman, the chemistry teacher at Yale; Noah Webster, the successful author of the *Blue-backed Speller*; and Eli Whitney, already famous for his invention of the cotton gin.

Jedediah and Elizabeth Morse came to live with their son in New Haven.

"Why did you give up the pulpit?" Lucretia asked.

Jedediah Morse's long hair had turned white. Now his eyes grew troubled. "I'd pastored the same congregation for thirty years," Jedediah said. "So when some of the people grew cool toward me, I decided not to seek another post."

"You could have stayed and fought," Samuel said. "The other members supported you."

"I could have stayed, but I determined it to be in the best interest of all concerned to step down."

Elizabeth said, "Your father wants to work on other matters. He plans to study the Northwest Indians."

Soon the whole Morse clan was living at the little cottage on Temple Street in New Haven. Even Nancy Shepherd came along as cook.

Samuel awoke to the pleasant aroma of buckwheat cakes. He dressed and joined the family around the breakfast table.

"What do you wish to drink?" Nancy asked.

"Hot cider," Sidney said.

"Coffee," Richard said.

"Tea," Samuel said. "Nancy, I've brought up rice and sweet potatoes from South Carolina. Would you be a dear and cook some tonight? I've developed a taste for Southern food."

Jedediah Morse, wearing his red robe, said, "I'll stay with clam chowder and lobster."

Every one talked at once. Samuel sat back and listened to the breakfast conversation. He caught Lucretia's eye. She seemed so lovely, her face aglow with the same joy he felt.

Perhaps tomorrow problems would come his way. But now, at this instant and in this room, nothing could dampen the warmth of the family reunion.

6

Breakfast in the White House

While in New Haven, David De Forest called upon Samuel with an unusual request. De Forest, an affluent merchant who had made his fortune in Buenos Aires, Argentina, wanted portraits of himself and of his wife. But—

"My wife and I differ in age by twenty-one years," David De Forest explained. "She is much younger than I am. I desire portraits to show us more nearly alike in age."

Samuel wrestled with the problem. His solution displayed complete mastery of his craft. He painted Mrs. De Forest at her actual age, arrayed in her lace, elegant pearl ornaments, and rich clothing.

Samuel painted her husband in strong light. The brightly lighted side of the face showed the vigor and strength of the man so that he appeared years younger. But on the other side of the face, in the shadows, Samuel filled in the hollow cheeks and tracery of wrinkles of the older man.

For many years, people singled out the De Forest portrait as one of Samuel F. B. Morse's greatest achievements.

In late fall of 1819, Samuel left again for South Carolina. This time Lucretia did not go with him. She stayed in New Haven to care for their first child, a daughter, Susan Walker Morse.

On the way to South Carolina, Samuel stopped in Washington for the painting sessions with President Monroe. Samuel intended to stay at a hotel in the city.

Elizabeth Monroe, the first lady, would have none of those plans. "The president can spare only ten or twenty minutes at a time. You'd be forever running between here and the hotel."

"What should I do?" Samuel asked.

"Mr. Morse, you are our honored guest," she said. "You can stay in the White House and set up your easel next to the president's conference room."

At ten o'clock in the morning, Samuel set up his easel and prepared his palette. He waited all day. Finally, at four o'clock, the president made his appearance.

President James Monroe was about six feet tall, but stoop-shouldered, his face prematurely lined. His grayish blue eyes were deep-set and kindly.

The president was in an expansive mood, affable and pleased with the progress he saw the country making. He described his time in office as an era of good feeling.

Samuel merely said, "Yes, Mr. President." He worked as quickly as good craftsmanship allowed.

Speaking more to himself than to Morse, the president said, "Work is underway on the Erie Canal to connect the Hudson River and Lake Erie. When it is finished, New York will become the most important city in the country."

"Even more important than Philadelphia or Boston?" Samuel asked.

"Yes, Mr. Morse. Great growth is in store for New York City."

An aide stepped into the room and whispered a message to the president.

"You must excuse me," President Monroe said. He strode from the room after only ten minutes.

The president seldom spent more than ten or twenty minutes at each sitting. Despite the frequent interruptions, Samuel managed to make progress on the portrait.

During his free time he saw the sights of Washington.

Charles Bulfinch, architect for the Capitol building, welcomed Samuel. "The United States is the only nation in the world to plan a capital exclusively for its seat of government," Bulfinch said.

Together the architect and artist walked along the great halls of Congress. Their steps on the marble floor echoed hollowly in the vast distances.

"In ten years the rotunda will join the two great halls," Bullfinch said.

"It is a splendid sight already," Samuel agreed.

During the week in Washington, Samuel dined with the president and the first lady. Samuel wanted to ask a favor of the president, and now the time seemed right. "For several years, my father—"

The president said, " 'Geography' Morse."

"Yes," Samuel said. "My father is well known, and for several years he had introduced me to community leaders across the country. Now I find myself in the unusual position of asking a favor in his behalf."

The president said, "What do you wish?"

"Father is coming to Washington in a few weeks," Samuel said. "He wishes to seek government assistance to study Northwest Indians. Father recently resigned his pulpit, and now he has time to undertake this work.''

''I will listen to his proposal,'' President Monroe promised. ''In turn, I have a favor to ask of you. Could you obtain some small elms from your home in New Haven?''

Rather baffled, Samuel agreed.

The president explained, ''I have been collecting trees from around the country and planting them on my estate in Oak Hill, Virginia. You would do me a service and an honor by sending me plantings of elms from New England.''

''I will see that Father brings them with him,'' Samuel promised.

After three weeks, Samuel finished the painting.

The president, his wife Elizabeth, and their two daughters were delighted with the portrait.

Samuel said, ''It will hang in the City Hall of Charleston.''

''You must make a copy for us,'' Elizabeth urged.

Samuel stayed a few more days in the White House to copy the portrait.

''I think I like it better than the one by Gilbert Stuart,'' the president confided.

Samuel, leaving the copy behind, went by stagecoach, rather than schooner, to South Carolina. The long and tedious overland trip was a preview of the problems he faced in Charleston. During the previous year his Uncle Finley had died. It was as if a bit of the light and joy in Charleston had gone out.

He stayed for a few weeks in one of Mrs. Muro's expensive rooms. But—

''I've decided to cut expenses and lodge in my painting room,'' he told Mrs. Muro.

''Is business bad?'' she asked.

"I'm afraid so," Samuel said. "I've received no new customers, and some who owe me have not paid."

Mrs. Muro tut-tutted. "Whatever can be the matter?"

Samuel knew the reason. "The quick paint artists have moved into Charleston. They make poorly executed and badly composed pictures at cut-rate prices."

One day a customer named Mrs. Ball swept into his studio to view a completed picture.

"It is beautiful," she said. Her children, one and all, grew excited at seeing their mother's image so exactly detailed.

The woman examined the painting at great length. "But something is wrong," she said. "The curtains in the background are brown. I prefer purple."

"Yes, Mrs. Ball," Samuel said. "I will repaint the curtains to be purple."

She came back the next day.

"No, it is still not right. Can it be altered?"

"Of course," Samuel said. He'd learned patience when dealing with customers.

"Very well," Mrs. Ball said. "I cannot bear the color of the guitar—and it's not the right shape."

"The guitar is an exact copy of the original," Samuel pointed out.

Mrs. Ball exploded. "Change the guitar! And put a gold chain around my neck."

"Yes, ma'am," Samuel said in exasperation.

Finally, Samuel painted in all of her changes. Yet she still wasn't satisfied.

"The portrait is frightful," Mrs. Ball complained. "I have no intention of paying the full amount."

That evening Samuel walked down to the harbor. Dejected and homesick, he watched a steamship being loaded. As it pulled away from the dock, Samuel had to fight the urge to jump aboard and return home.

That night he wrote, "Dearest Lucrece, I miss you and little Susan more than you can think. I long to have us all together at New Haven. Someday I'll be able to stay home with you, and we'll have no more goodbyes."

Samuel spent the winters of 1819 and 1820 in Charleston. But the city had nothing more to offer the painter. He packed his belongings and went home with no intention of returning.

During Samuel's absence, Lucretia had quietly taken on the numerous household duties. With relief, she threw herself into his arms for a tearful reunion.

In the spring of 1821, the little cottage on Temple Street in New Haven harbored the three brothers—Samuel, age thirty; Sidney, age twenty-seven; Richard, age twenty-six—as well as Jedediah Morse. All of the Morses, father and sons, were without regular income. The family affairs needed serious attention.

"Let's go for a walk," Samuel suggested to his wife.

They walked along the street, enjoying the signs of spring—robins hopping across the green lawns, white oaks full of new foliage, and the pleasant smell of mountain laurel in flower.

Lucretia said, "Although your father has the Indian commission, he earns only a meager salary from it."

Samuel stopped and looked at her. His heart melted when he saw the concern in her eyes. "Everything will be all right," he assured her.

"I . . . I learned that your father has been borrowing money. Last week he began packing some of the books from his library."

"Whatever for?" Samuel asked.

"He intends to sell them at auction to raise money!"

Samuel was shocked. "The books are the tools of his trade."

Samuel tried to help his father, but the proud old gentleman would not think of being a burden to his son.

After a few months in New Haven, Samuel realized his success in South Carolina had been a cruel false dawn. Once again he eked out an existence, painting portraits at a fraction of their real worth.

With her customary fortitude, Lucretia readily accepted the hard times. She encouraged Samuel to pursue his serious painting.

"You could continue as a portrait painter," Lucretia said. "But your great canvas is still rolled up in the cellar and gathering dust."

Samuel grew thoughtful. He had carried the empty canvas all the way from England with the hope of one day painting a great scene from American history.

Lucretia's eyes showed the intensity of her feeling. "You must act now, or you may never have the opportunity again. Paint the big picture before the money we have saved is gone."

"You're right," Samuel agreed. "The times call for a dramatic change in plans. Rembrandt Peale is showing his *Court of Death* to good crowds. The American public may now be ready for something more than portraits."

"So we agree you should begin a great canvas," Lucretia said. "But of what?"

"Not paintings of Greek gods or mythical figures," Samuel said. He recalled the dismal failure of his exhibit of the *Judgment of Jupiter* and the *Dying Hercules.*

Samuel remembered the vast expanse of the Capitol building. He said, "I'll portray democracy in action—a painting of the House of Representatives in session.''

In November of 1821, Samuel once again said goodbye to Lucretia and traveled to Washington.

President Monroe welcomed Samuel to Washington. ''I've instructed Mr. Bullfinch to help you in whatever way he can,'' the president said.

Samuel presented Charles Bullfinch with a special gift, one of the *Dying Hercules* statues.

''I made a mold from the original clay model and cast a half dozen copies from it,'' Samuel said. ''I brought the mold with me from England, but a man cleaning the house thought the parts to be broken plaster. He threw them away while I was in South Carolina.''

''So this is one of the only remaining copies?'' Bullfinch asked.

''Yes,'' Samuel said.

''How can I ever repay you?'' Bullfinch asked.

Samuel said, ''When it comes time to choose an artist to paint scenes for the panels in the Capitol Rotunda, remember me.''

Bullfinch agreed. ''But that is still several years away. In the meantine, I'll see you have a room in the Capitol as your studio.''

Congressmen welcomed Samuel's idea of a painting showing them in action. They came to his studio in a lower room in the Capitol to sit for the sketches.

By the middle of December, Samuel was working sixteen hours a day. He wrote to Lucretia, ''I am up at daylight, have my breakfast and prayers over, and then begin the labors.''

One of his sitters was the flamboyant John Randolph of Virginia.

Samuel held a cup of tea in one hand and sipped from it as he penciled a sketch of the congressman.

Samuel said, "I plan to make rough sketches here in Washington, and combine them into a single painting when I return to New Haven."

"How is it going?" John Randolph asked.

"Well enough," Samuel said. "The real problem is the hall itself. An interesting design for placing the figures in the room has escaped me. It is as if the hall is too vast to be reduced to canvas."

Samuel sketched the room time and again. Each time he discarded the drawing and started afresh.

One evening he arrived as the doorkeeper lowered the brass chandelier and lighted the thirty lamps. As the doorkeeper raised the chandelier, it cast the hall in a soft, subdued light.

"This is it," Samuel said to the doorkeeper. "The lighting is mysterious and enchanting, yet effective. May I paint here at night?"

The doorman hesitated.

"I'll put you in the painting," Samuel promised.

The doorkeeper quickly agreed to keep the hall lighted for an extra two hours.

Samuel painted the great domed room lighted by the huge brass chandelier. He placed the eighty figures in small groups as they studied bills and worked late into the night.

By February of 1822 Samuel finished his work in Washington.

He mailed a letter to Lucretia telling her he was packing to leave Washington. He was so anxious to return home, he rode the stagecoach straight through, making the trip from Washington to New Haven in only six days. He arrived before his letter!

After finishing *Representative Hall*, he gave Lucretia a sneak preview of the painting.

"Why there's your father—and an Indian chief," she said.

Samuel explained, "Father came to Washington to hear the reading of his Indian Commission report. A Pawnee chief was visiting Washington, so I put them in the upper gallery."

Samuel opened his painting on Market Street in Boston. Art critics praised *Representative Hall*, but the crowds stayed away.

Samuel had passed beyond competition with Gilbert Stuart and the other artists. Now he competed with the many popular attractions in Boston—music concerts, traveling road shows of strange and wonderful animals from around the world, opera companies, and dozens of other events.

After three weeks, Samuel opened the ledger and added the attendance figures. During the first week three hundred people paid admission, the next week only one hundred, and this week—

Samuel paused and looked out the window at the slow, cold rain falling. During the entire day only three people had come in.

After making sure the fire in the wood stove was out, he closed the studio and locked the door. Tomorrow he would put the *Representative Hall* in storage and notify the landlord to close the studio.

As the year dragged on, Samuel could not stay inactive. He and Sidney worked together on their invention of an improved water pump. The house in New Haven became even more crowded by the clutter of wheels and pistons.

Lucretia disapproved of the mess, especially since it took Samuel away from his painting.

Samuel spoke in defense of the project. "The pump will be used for fire engines and by boats to pump out the bilge."

Lucretia was not convinced. "Your future is as an artist, not as an inventor," she said.

Samuel said, "I'll be making drawings tonight."

Lucretia looked more pleased. Then she asked, "Of whom?"

"Not whom," Samuel said. "Of what. My special skill in the pump project is to make the drawings that will be used in applying for a patent. The pump is a 'hare and tortoise' enterprise."

"Hare and tortoise?" Lucretia asked, puzzled.

Samuel explained how he and Sidney had come by those names. "Father gave the nicknames to us," Samuel said.

Lucretia nodded. "Your father is an accurate judge of character. You have become one of the best known character portrait painters in America, yet you spend your time—"

"This is different," Samuel said. "Eli Whitney thinks the design of the pump is a good one. He said it is simple and much less expensive than those in common use."

Lucretia pleaded with her husband, "Yesterday I

watched as you demonstrated the pump. I overheard a man in the crowd speak. He said, 'Mr. Morse better stick to his brush.' He's right, you know.''

"But I feel miserable in doing nothing," Samuel said. "The last few months in New Haven have been awful. I've made only a few paintings, of Eli Whitney, Professor Silliman, Jeremiah Day and a few other neighbors.''

"Don't forget Noah Webster," Lucretia said. "He will use your portrait of him as the frontispiece of his *American Dictionary of the English Language*. Your work will be put before many thousands of people.''

Samuel could not argue with her. He knew Lucretia to be correct.

"New York," Samuel said. "I'll open a studio in New York. That city is destined to become the crossroads of America.''

"New York?" Lucretia asked. "Where did you hear such an outlandish idea?''

"From a highly placed source," Samuel said. "The president himself is certain the Erie Canal will make New York a window to the nation. If I am to succeed at all, it will be in New York.''

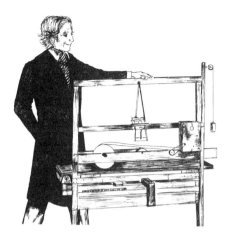

7

The Final Goodbye

Before going to New York, Samuel proposed taking a short vacation with Benjamin Silliman into the Berkshire Hills of western Massachusetts. Silliman had been suffering from a persistent cold.

"A change of scenery will help you shake the cold," Samuel said.

Silliman agreed. "But why do the Berkshires interest you?"

Samuel said, "The trip will be my last chance to paint landscapes before going back to portraits full-time."

Once in the mountains, Benjamin Silliman rested in a patch of sunlight as Samuel painted the scene—rolling highlands dominated by wooded ridges.

While Samuel painted, Benjamin Silliman read from the Bible. After a moment he said thoughtfully, "This must be the most beautiful part of the United States. With the Bible in my hands, and this scene before me, I see a perfect harmony between science and religion."

Samuel agreed. "Beauty like this lifts the heart from nature up to nature's God. When I look to God, He calms my fears about the future. I seem to hear a voice saying, 'If I clothe the lilies of the field, shall I not also clothe you?' "

One trait people instantly saw in Samuel Morse was a childlike faith in God. When things were the darkest, he would say, "Why should I expect my sky to be never clouded, my sun to be never darkened? I've enjoyed the sunshine of prosperity far more than most people."

At his evening devotions, Samuel developed the habit of reviewing the day's activity. He would ask himself, "Have I received a particular blessing today and not been thankful for it?" This self-examination became a lifelong habit.

Wherever he went, Samuel sought out the Christians in the community to be with them. He accepted the Holy Bible as the guide and rule of his life. Samuel put his religious beliefs into action by working to start Sunday schools. To his surprise he found that some people opposed the idea of schools for children on Sunday.

He and Benjamin Silliman packed their saddlebags and mounted the horses. "Why would anyone oppose a Sunday school?" Samuel asked.

Benjamin Silliman said, "It's a new idea which frightens some people. But I agree with the person who said, 'The soul of freedom is true religion exerting its moral power on an educated population.' "

"Who said that?" Samuel asked.

"You did, my friend," Silliman answered, "when you spoke to convince the church in New Haven to start the Sunday school."

Due to Samuel's efforts, New Haven began a Sunday school, one of the first in the United States. Samuel served as the superintendent.

He also made donations to schools for the training of preachers and ministers. For instance, at the time when his financial affairs reached their lowest, he donated five hundred dollars to Yale College, probably the largest donation compared to the poverty of the giver which that institution ever received.

In the fall of 1824, Morse again said goodbye to Lucretia, Susan and little Charles, and left for New York.

In New York he stepped from the stagecoach, stretched, and looked around. He'd decided to locate his studio in the best part of the city, even if it meant cutting expenses elsewhere.

Up and down the city streets he trudged, past pigs rooting for throwaway food, through knots of recently arrived Irish immigrants, and across trenches cut into the streets for pipes to carry gas to light the city.

The second day saw him in Manhattan. Men in tail coats and top hats strolled along Broadway, arm in arm with women in bonnets and parasols.

Samuel slowed his steps. He walked past Trinity Church at the head of Wall Street. Nearby was Trumbull's American Academy of Fine Arts, and Wiley's Bookshop, a gathering place for young artists and literary men.

"This is the place," Samuel decided. He opened his studio at 96 Broadway.

Samuel's two brothers, Sidney and Richard, had come to New York the year before. They'd launched the *New York Observer*, a religious weekly newspaper. Samuel visited their offices and put an advertisement in their paper announcing the opening of his studio.

"You've settled in an expensive part of the city," Sidney observed.

"Yes, I know," Samuel said, "but I was fortunate to find a fine room on Broadway opposite Trinity

Church for my studio. I'll sleep on the floor and put my mattress out of sight during the day.''

"It sounds pretty bleak," Richard said.

Samuel didn't deny it. "I do long for a permanent home and steady employment so Lucretia and the children can be with me."

Early in 1825, John Quincy Adams would be sworn into office as the sixth president of the United States. General Lafayette, the French hero of the American War of Independence, was invited to attend the ceremonies and visit the country as the guest of the nation.

When Lafayette arrived in New York, the city gave him a hero's welcome. The roar of cannon salutes, the peal of church bells, and flag-draped steamboats greeted the ship carrying Lafayette.

The city council asked Lafayette to sit for a portrait to hang in city hall.

Artists pressed forward with their qualifications to paint the portrait. Samuel entered the intense competition, too. But he felt his own chances to be slim because he'd been in the city only a few months.

In January of 1825, Samuel made a quick trip back to New Haven. He came to see Finley, his newborn son and to announce the good news. "I have been chosen to paint the portrait of Lafayette."

"Oh, Samuel, that is marvelous," Lucretia said.

Samuel said, "It will mean the long delayed event—a home together. In less than a year there will be no more goodbyes."

Lucretia hugged Samuel. "No more goodbyes," she said wistfully.

Samuel's sitting with Lafayette had been arranged in Washington. In February, he reached the capital and took a room in Gadsby's Hotel where Lafayette lodged. Samuel dashed off a letter to Lucretia. He wanted her to share in his success, so he promised to describe the people and events in his letters home.

Back in New Haven, Connecticut, Rebecca Webster visited Lucretia Morse. Suddenly Lucretia twitched in pain and put a hand to her side. "Oh!"

"Here," Rebecca Webster said and took her arm. "Are you all right?"

"I think so," Lucretia said, rather dazed.

"Let me help you to bed," Rebecca said. "I'll take care of Susan and Charles and put baby Finley in the hands of Nancy Shepherd."

Lucretia, feeling weak and looking pale, allowed herself to be put into bed.

Samuel, of course, had no way of knowing about her sudden illness. He finished the letter in pleasant anticipation of meeting Lafayette.

Some artists described the general's features as homely and difficult to paint. Would Lafayette be a battle-weary old soldier, befuddled and doughy faced? It would be a challenge to make a tired old man look like a national hero.

The two met for breakfast.

Samuel realized that he faced a new challenge. How could he possibly capture the strength and character of the man—the face that combined humility and nobility, the firm lips, thrusting jaw, and intense eyes?

Samuel was overcome by awe and respect. He stood speechless in the presence of the great man.

Lafayette acted first. He strode forward, took Samuel's hand and said, "Sir, I am exceedingly happy to meet you, especially on such an occasion."

Samuel regained his voice. "I . . . The honor is mine to paint the man who has spent his time and fortune in the support of liberty."

Lafayette laughed a rich, honest laugh that boomed through the room. "Your father made a geography of the country, and now you'll make a geography of my face!"

That night Samuel wrote to Lucretia, "I am making progress with the general. He is interested in everything, and seems to know everybody. He remembers Professor Silliman and others in New Haven with great affection."

During that same afternoon in New Haven, Lucretia rose to have her bed freshly made. She chatted with the maid, cheerfully looking toward being with Samuel in their own house in New York.

Lucretia lay back down. She shivered as if chilled and closed her eyes.

Five minutes later Jedediah Morse came into the room to say good night. He immediately saw something was terribly wrong.

"Call Dr. Smith," he told the maid. "Hurry!"

As Samuel finished his letter in Washington, the

doctor in New Haven pulled the sheet over Lucretia's head. ''She's gone,'' the doctor said.

The next day at the sitting, Samuel could not shake the sense of history wrapped in the man before him. Samuel thought: This is the man now before me, the very man, who was the friend and companion of George Washington, who is the terror of tyrants, who suffered in the dungeon, the man both America and France call the father of freedom.

Lafayette told about his wife, Adrienne. They'd met and married while teenagers and remained life-long sweethearts. She'd stayed by his side, even going to the dungeon with him, until death took her away. As Lafayette told about her, his eyes softened and a quiver came to his voice.

Yes, Samuel thought, this man understands about love as well as about war.

On his last night in Washington, Samuel dressed to attend President Monroe's farewell reception. Samuel rode to the White House with James Fenimore Cooper, the celebrated author of the *Leatherstocking Tales*.

During their conversation, Fenimore Cooper learned that Samuel Morse had graduated from Yale.

''I went to Yale, too,'' Cooper said. ''But they asked me to leave.''

''Whatever for?'' Samuel asked.

Cooper grinned. ''I opened a tutor's door—with a charge of gunpowder.''

Samuel shook his head. Explode gunpowder inside the halls of Yale! Unthinkable! But not unthinkable for Cooper. He possessed a quicksilver mind that darted from one topic to another, always with an opinion, never at a loss for words.

Despite their nearly opposite characters, Samuel Morse and Fenimore Cooper became instant friends.

President Monroe greeted them at the White House. At the reception were John Quincy Adams and his vice-president, John C. Calhoun.

"Uh-oh," Cooper whispered. "Here comes Jackson."

Of the four men who'd run for president, Andrew Jackson won the most votes, but not enough to be the clear victor. The House of Representatives made the final decision and chose Adams, rather than Jackson, as president.

As Andrew Jackson walked toward John Quincy Adams, a hush came over the crowd. They wondered what would happen when the two men met face to face for the first time since the election.

John Quincy Adams waited, cool and aloof. Andrew Jackson cordially took his hand and congratulated him upon his election. The crowd breathed again.

Cooper said, ''Look at Adams. He's the most uncomfortable man here.''

Samuel said, ''Everyone else is having a fine time, even Jackson. This will be something to write home about.''

The next morning Samuel's mail arrived as he ate breakfast in the hotel. Expecting a letter from Lucretia, he found one from his father instead.

Why did Father write, but not Lucretia? Samuel opened the letter and began reading.

''My beloved son,'' Jedediah Morse wrote. ''My heart is in pain and deeply sorrowful, while I announce to you the sudden and unexpected death of your dearly loved wife.''

Samuel's vision failed, blinded by tears.

Samuel confessed to Lafayette that he could not work on the portrait. ''The thought of seeing my dear Lucretia, and returning home to her, served always to give me fresh courage. Now I hardly know what to substitute in her place.''

Lafayette understood because he, too, had lost a young and beautiful wife. ''I want to tell you how deeply I sympathize in your grief. When I find myself again near you, you can finish it.''

Samuel read Jedediah's letter through again. It had been more than a week coming to him. While he dined with the famous and powerful people of Washington, Lucretia took sick and died without his even being aware of her distress.

Heart-broken, Samuel returned to New York. All he could do was ask for the prayers of his family and his Christian friends. In his loneliness, he brought Susan to live with him, only to discover that he could not look after her. She went back to Nancy Shepherd and Grandmother Morse in New Haven.

Samuel finished the Lafayette portrait. It showed the old soldier against a glowing sunset sky. Because of Samuel's own grief, the portrait caught a great sadness in Lafayette's features. Those who viewed the painting came away with a sense of history, as if the portrait showed not only the man but the events in his life as well. The painting established Samuel Morse as America's foremost portrait painter.

Success came to Samuel. Success—but no Lucretia. The money to buy a house—but no wife to make it a home. Even after a year, Samuel daily felt the pain of her loss. He slept fitfully and began taking long walks to try to forget his sorrows.

Early one morning, as Samuel came back from one of his walks, he noticed Thomas Cummings and Fred Agate, two poor art students, at the door of the Academy of Arts.

"Hello, boys," Samuel said. "Why are you waiting outside?"

"The door is still locked," Cummings said.

"It is eight already," Samuel said. "The Academy should be open. Knock on the door."

"It is useless," Agate said. "We'll be ignored."

"But the whole purpose of the Academy is to help beginning artists," Samuel pointed out.

Cummings said, "Colonel Trumbull only opens the doors when he feels like it." Dispirited, the two young men turned away.

At that moment Colonel Trumbull arrived at the Academy. Samuel questioned the man about turning the two artists away.

"The Academy is for young *gentlemen*," Colonel Trumbull said. He looked at Morse, but raised his voice so the two poor students could overhear. "Cummings and Agate must remember that *beggars* are not to be choosers."

Thomas Cummings caught Samuel's eye and shrugged as if to say, "We told you so."

Samuel saw the need for a friendly place for poor artists to meet and learn their craft. He began conducting classes at the Academy.

Trumbell resented the meetings. He waited until Samuel was away and stalked into the room. "Sign this roll book," Trumbull ordered the students.

Cummings looked at the roll book. "This says our meetings are part of the American Academy—that we are your students."

"I'm leaving the book for your signatures," Trumbull said haughtily.

The boys refused to sign the book. Instead they banded together and urged Samuel to start a new school.

He threw himself into the task, and began the National Academy of Design to help deserving but poor artists. With a rousing cheer, the artists elected Samuel president of the Academy.

That evening Samuel walked back to his studio with a spring in his step and a glow in his heart. He slept soundly for the first time in months. Samuel had put his life back to normal—not by dwelling on his own misery, but by helping others overcome theirs.

During this time, Samuel attended a series of public lectures on electricity and magnetism. Professor Freeman Dana of Columbia College delivered the lectures. He demonstrated his points by operating an electromagnet made of wire wrapped around an iron bar bent in the shape of a horseshoe. When Dana threw the switch, electricity flowed through the wire and the iron bar became a powerful magnet.

Professor Dana was as enthusiastic about electricity as Silliman had been. Professor Dana ended his lectures, "I foresee great and wonderful benefits for mankind when the forces of electricity are fully understood.''

The power of the electromagnet and the fact it could be turned on and off impressed Samuel the most.

The lectures on electromagnetism attracted Samuel's interest for a time. But painting continued to be his main concern. For many years he'd wanted to study more of the paintings of the great masters. Most of these paintings hung in museums, churches, and art galleries in Europe. By the fall of 1828 Samuel Morse saw little reason to delay the trip. Few ties kept him home. His father had died two years before and his mother earlier that year.

He found a home for Susan with her aunt and namesake, Susan Walker Pickering in Concord, New Hampshire. The boys, Charles and Finley, he placed with his brother Richard, who had just married and lived in the family home in New Haven.

Samuel Morse sailed from New York on November 8, 1829, and landed at Liverpool twenty-six days later. He lodged at the King's Arms Hotel, the same hotel where he had stayed when he arrived as a student in England eighteen years earlier.

He looked up Charles Leslie, and met his roommate in warm friendship; he studied the priceless art collections in the Vatican in Rome; he visited Paris for a reunion with Lafayette.

The next year found him in the great hall of the Louvre, making copies of the paintings in that world-famous museum. As he concentrated on his painting, a raucous voice interrupted.

''Lay it on here, Samuel,'' the voice said, ''more yellow. The nose is too short, the eyes too small. If I were a painter, what a picture I would paint!''

''Cooper!'' Samuel said. ''What are you doing in Paris?''

''Enjoying myself,'' James Fenimore Cooper said,

"and writing a book—*The Last of the Mohicans*."

Another man of note whom Morse met in Paris was Baron Alexander von Humboldt, the famous naturalist. Baron von Humboldt was a larger-than-life figure and a world traveler. He was an amateur artist, too, and he frequently met with Fenimore Cooper in the Louvre to watch Samuel work.

The topic of conversation was the fall of Warsaw, Poland to the Russian army. The news came by way of the French semaphore system, a method of signaling messages by means of towers with jointed arms that moved up or down. The signal arms could be seen on hills far away by observers with telescopes. The observers relayed the message from one mountaintop to the next.

"The mail in America is too slow," Fenimore Cooper said. "We need something like the French semaphore."

Baron von Humboldt said, "The semaphore was tried in America, but it didn't work."

Samuel Morse spoke. "It's not fast enough. Lightning would serve us better."

"Lightning?" Fenimore Cooper asked. "I've always seen Samuel Morse as a sober-minded, commonsense sort of fellow. But he talks about lightning as if it could actually be used to signal messages!"

Baron von Humboldt said, "He's talking about electricity, which is a tame form of lightning. Franklin, Oersted, Ampere, Volta, and myself have all experimented with it—so far electricity has remained merely a plaything of science."

Samuel said, "Twenty-five years have passed since I saw my first electric demonstrations. Yet, even today it remains a plaything of science. Will it always be so?"

8

Aboard the Sully

Samuel boarded the packet ship *Sully* at Havre, France, on October 1, 1832, to sail for New York. The *Sully*, a small and speedy vessel, carried mail across the Atlantic Ocean. Like other packet ships, she carried a few passengers as well.

Captain Pell welcomed Samuel to the *Sully* and introduced him to the other passengers: Mr. Fisher, a Philadelphia lawyer; William C. Rives, the American ambassador to France; and others.

"You must meet one other passenger," Captain Pell said. "Dr. Charles T. Jackson is a young medical doctor from Boston. He is going home to America after learning the latest medical treatments in Paris."

Young Dr. Jackson had learned the latest fashions as well, and dressed as a dandy in striped trousers and a broad-skirted coat.

Samuel's spirits rose. His fellow passengers proved to be an amusing and friendly group. The promise of lively dinner table conversation meant the voyage would go quickly.

True, he would arrive in America practically penniless. Never mind! Samuel Morse was forty-one years old and a famous painter. The days of hard poverty lay behind him. Now he could look forward to a career surrounded by friends and honored by his fellow artists.

Although Samuel did enjoy the long conversations aboard ship, he stayed in the background. He was content to sit back and enjoy the ideas being tossed back and forth by the other passengers. The conversation turned to electricity and magnetism.

Mr. Fisher asked, ''Is the flow of electricity slowed by the length of a wire?''

''No,'' Dr. Charles T. Jackson said. He brimmed with facts he'd learned in Paris about the most recent scientific discoveries. ''Benjamin Franklin is reported to have passed current through many miles of wire. He observed no difference of time between the touch at one end and the spark at the other.''

Samuel sat up suddenly, as if struck by an electric spark. ''If this is so and the presence of electricity can be made visible in any desired part of the circuit, I see no reason why information might not be instantly sent by electricity to any distance.''

''That may be,'' Dr. Jackson said. He turned back to the dinner table conversation.

The thought captured Samuel's imagination. Could signals be sent instantly anywhere along a wire by electricity? Could a message be sent from New Haven to Washington in an instant rather than in a week? Could a wire be laid across the Atlantic ocean floor? Why, newspapers in America could carry news of events that had taken place that very morning in Europe.

But how? How would an electric signaling device work?

"It can be done!" Samuel said.

The men around the table looked at Morse, puzzled by his outburst, and by the burning gleam in his eyes.

He withdrew from the cabin and paced the ship's deck. Thoughts raced through his mind. Feverishly he drew one of his sketchbooks from his pocket. He forced himself to calm down, to think carefully and logically, and to write down his idea.

An idea is not enough, he realized. It must be expressed in terms of wire, magnets, and batteries. He worked on his new idea all day and far into the night.

Samuel found himself in the middle of the ocean with a burning idea—and no reference books to check his facts. He struggled to remember what he'd learned in the classes of Professors Jeremiah Day and Benjamin Silliman, from the demonstrations of Professor Dana, and from his own reading about electricity and magnetism.

Carefully, Samuel recorded what he knew about electricity. The battery Volta invented generates electricity. Copper wire conducts electricity. According to Jackson, the speed of electricity through a circuit of wire is very fast. It is not slowed by the length of the wire.

Samuel hesitated. Could Jackson be mistaken? Perhaps electricity did slow down after a few miles. Well, he'd assume Jackson to be correct for now, and test it later himself.

Next, Samuel wrote down what he knew about magnetism. An electric magnet can be made by bending a bar of iron into the shape of a horseshoe and wrapping it in coils of wire. The bar becomes a strong magnet when electricity flows, but loses the magnetism when the current stops. An electric magnet can be turned on and off by a switch from anywhere along the electric circuit, even miles away.

Samuel instantly grasped the task before him. He thought, ''The message will be sent by switching a circuit on and off. At the other end an electromagnet will receive the message and write it out. But how?''

He filled his notebook with dozens of drawings. After several sleepless nights, he worked out the details. In his final design, electricity flowed through a circuit of wire and caused an electromagnet to raise and lower a metal lever. A pencil attached to the lever marked dots and dashes on a moving strip of paper.

He showed the drawing to Mr. Fisher at the breakfast table. ''In France I saw their system for signaling at a distance—a semaphore. My invention will be for writing at a distance—a telegraph. The magnet is controlled by electricity and writes on a strip of paper. The pencil mark can be one sign, the lack of a mark another sign, the length of the mark a third sign. The marks write a code of dots and dashes.''

Samuel waited for Mr. Fisher to give his opinion of the invention.

Slowly Mr. Fisher nodded. ''Yes, I understand how it could work. But tell me, Mr. Morse, what makes this idea so important to you?''

How could Samuel explain? Because of the lack of speedy communication, England and the United States had blundered into a war which need not have been declared, and they fought a bloody battle in New Orleans after signing a peace treaty. Because of the lack of quick and dependable communication, Lucretia had died and been buried before he even learned that she'd become ill. Those reasons alone justified the telegraph.

Finally, Samuel said, ''I believe God created the great forces of nature, not only to show His infinite power, but to express His good will to man. God created the forces of nature for the benefit of mankind, if we can only discover how to use them.''

Mr. Fisher, Ambassador Rives, and Dr. Jackson all listened politely to Samuel's proposal for the telegraph. Clearly, they saw his telegraph as merely a pen-and-paper idea. It meant nothing more to them than the dozens of other ideas they'd tossed about during the voyage.

"But this is real," Samuel said. However, they'd moved on to other matters.

Ruefully, he realized sketching a telegraph was far easier than making one. The corner hardware store sold no electromagnets, no batteries, and no insulated wire. A blacksmith would have to be hired to bend an iron rod to the proper shape. Wire would have to be wound by hand and insulated with silk or cotton ribbon.

The *Sully* landed in New York harbor on November 16, 1832. Captain Pell shook hands with his passengers.

Samuel strode to the gangplank. "Well, Captain," he said, and tapped his notebook, "should you hear of the telegraph one of these days, as the wonder of the world, remember the discovery was made on board the good ship *Sully*."

Samuel disembarked at the wharf at the foot of Rector Street. Sidney and Richard waited for him.

Richard, the more serious of the brothers, expected Samuel to be bubbling with details of his travels and the great paintings he expected to execute upon his return home. Instead, Samuel flipped open the notebook and showed them the diagrams and notes.

"During the voyage, I made an important invention that will astonish the world," Samuel predicted. "The telegraph is a way to communicate by means of electricity. The dots and spaces make it possible—"

Richard, rather irritated, asked, "But what of your career as an artist?"

Samuel said, "I could earn a good living as a painter. But for my invention to succeed, I should give full time to it."

Richard compressed his lips in a thin line of disapproval. Rather stiffly he said, "Let's collect your baggage. You can stay with me until you find a place of your own."

Samuel sensed that Richard wanted to hear no more about the telegraph. "New York seems to be as I left it," Samuel commented. "Everybody is driving after money, as usual, and there is a fire alarm every half-hour, as usual, and the pigs have the freedom of the city, as usual."

Sidney laughed, "Except they are not the *same* people that are driving after money, nor the *same* houses burnt, nor the *same* pigs at large in the streets."

Richard's wife, Louisa, welcomed Samuel to her home for a reunion with his children. Much to her dismay, Samuel began his experiments immediately, melting lead over the fireplace to make parts of the telegraph.

"Samuel Finley Breese Morse!" Louisa cried. "What are you doing! The carpet is afire!"

"Ah . . ." Samuel set down the mold, and stamped out the smoldering carpet.

Louisa cried again. "The chair is afire!"

Samuel picked up the hot mold, which had scorched the cane-bottom chair.

She stamped her feet, aghast at the hole burned in the loose carpeting. "This must stop," she said. "I will not have my home turned into a laboratory."

Samuel apologized profusely. "But I must experiment to make the apparatus."

"Not here," Louisa said firmly.

Richard said, "Sidney and I have a spare room on the fifth story of the newspaper building. If Samuel is agreeable, he can have that room."

Samuel agreed, of course. The little room became his studio, bedroom, kitchen, and workshop. On one side of the room stood a narrow cot on which he slept—when sleep overcame his strict regimen of experiments.

He made the first telegraph from an empty picture frame fastened to a table. The wheels of an old wooden clock carried the paper forward. Because of the makeshift quality of the contraption, he dared show it only to Sidney.

''The saw-toothed type makes and breaks the circuit so as to send dots and dashes on the paper. Only a single circuit is used.''

''Wire is cheap,'' Sidney interrupted. ''Wouldn't it be better to have twenty-six wires, each wire to represent a letter of the alphabet?''

''No,'' Samuel said. ''A single circuit will serve the purpose and is much simpler. Simplicity is better.''

Sidney looked at the complex collection of gears, wheels, and weights. The contraption could hardly be described as simple.

Samuel dismissed the telegraph model attached to the table. "This is only to test the idea. I'll make a better model before presenting it to the public."

The need for money to perfect the telegraph forced Samuel to accept a few sitters. He chose assignments which could be executed quickly.

One day he painted the finishing touches to an oil-on-canvas portrait of George Hyde Clarde. Luckily, the man had worn a black short coat. The inky blackness of the coat hid details, and he could paint it quickly. The buttons, too, he painted as nothing more than featureless black circles. On the face, however, he expended most of his efforts. He mixed paints to match exactly the skin color and milky blue eyes of Mr. Clarde.

The clatter of someone running up the steps interrupted his work. Fenimore Cooper burst into the room. "Look at this, Samuel!" He held a newspaper and waved it around. "It's about the Rotunda pictures."

"I know about them," Samuel said. "Four large panels in the great dome of the Capitol in Washington are still to be painted. A committee of Congress will select the artists to paint the pictures."

"You're the logical choice," Fenimore Cooper said. "Even Washington Allston has refused to be considered. He says you are the most deserving."

Samuel nodded. He did expect to be selected. "I feel my chances to be selected are good."

"Not anymore," Cooper said. "Can you believe this?" He thrust the newspaper before Samuel's startled eyes. "John Quincy Adams is a member of the selection committee. He says foreign artists should be allowed to compete."

"Why?" Samuel asked, baffled.

Fenimore Cooper read from the news account, "According to Adams, American artists aren't talented enough to execute such monumental works."

Samuel could not believe his ears. "I've a mind to answer Mr. Adams with a letter in the *Evening Post*."

"I've already written a reply," Fenimore Cooper said.

Fenimore Cooper wrote a particularly caustic letter. It appeared in the paper without his signature. Many people, including Adams himself, thought Samuel Morse had written the letter. Rather than helping Samuel, the letter did much to provoke Adams. Irritated, he passed over Samuel Morse and instead chose four other artists.

One of the artists selected was Henry Inman, a fellow member of the Academy of Design. Inman offered to resign from his commission provided Morse would be selected instead. Adams refused.

Humiliated and terribly disappointed, Samuel's interest in art faded. He looked upon his failure to be selected as the second greatest tragedy in his life. The death of his wife Lucretia was first, of course. Later, however, he marked the event as the turning point in his work on the telegraph. He threw himself fully into the task of perfecting it.

To conceal his poverty he took groceries to his room after dark and cooked his own meals. For lunch he frequently ate nothing more than tea and crackers.

During these dark days, Samuel's spirits lifted when the newly formed University of New York City asked him to serve as chairman of the art department. The position carried more prestige than pay. In fact, he drew no salary at all. Instead, he lectured occasionally and earned some money by tutoring private students.

But the new position did carry one attraction. The University assigned him a spacious room in the new University Building looking out on Washington Square. The room made a perfect laboratory. Around its walls he coiled seventeen hundred feet of wire—more than a quarter mile in length.

One day Samuel walked through Clinton Hall where the art students worked. He pointed out the strengths and weaknesses in their drawings. The students listened carefully, for Samuel demonstrated a ready grasp of the most intricate details of good painting. But . . .

"What occupies his mind?" a student whispered.

Another student shook his head sadly. "He spends his days alone in his room building some sort of electric piano."

The telegraph did faintly resemble a musical instrument. He sent messages by pressing a pianolike keyboard.

There, alone in his room, he sent a test message. The keys clicked, the wires hummed, the pencil raised and lowered, the paper rolled. The telegraph worked!

"Look, it works!" Samuel jumped up, holding the strip of paper. The four walls of the empty room were not impressed. Painfully, he was brought back to reality. The telegraph worked, but he alone knew about his success.

9

Gale and Vail

One of Samuel's friends at the University of New York was Leonard D. Gale, a professor of geology and mineralogy. Gale was a quiet, self-possessed man. He spoke in a calm, but confident voice. Although not easily impressed, he could inspire others and bring out the best in them.

In January of 1836, Samuel Morse invited Professor Gale to see the telegraph in operation for the first time. "You may not believe in my idea, Professor Gale," Samuel said, "but at least you will not laugh at it."

Samuel ushered Professor Gale into the large room and through the clutter of tools, coils of wire, bottles of sulfuric acid, and parts of batteries. Out of the way in one corner he'd put the keyboard version of the telegraph.

"I discarded the keyboard device as too clumsy. My experiments convinced me a single key is best for opening and closing the circuit."

Samuel sent a message through the telegraph for Professor Gale's benefit. "I have decided to call it the

American Electro-Magnetic Telegraph. I want everyone to know that an American invented it.''

Professor Gale instantly grasped what Samuel was trying to do. ''Why haven't you shown this to others?''

''I decided against presenting the telegraph at a public showing. Even if it worked flawlessly, the crude appearance of the device would not impress the average person. When I do present it to the public it will be as a finished device, complete and fully developed in every way.''

''During the last few weeks I've been sending messages over longer and longer lengths of wire. I wanted to test whether the current slows as the distance increases.''

''Does it?'' Professor Gale asked.

''No. The messages flash instantly through any length of wire.''

''Then what is the problem?''

''The current becomes weaker. The longer the wire, the weaker the current. Eventually it becomes too weak to operate the magnet at the other end,'' Samuel said. ''I've designed a relay to strengthen the current, although I haven't actually made one yet.''

''Perhaps a relay will not be necessary,'' Professor Gale said. ''Let me examine your telegraph in detail.''

After making a thorough study of the telegraph, Professor Leonard D. Gale offered two suggestions to improve the device. ''The number of turns of wires around the magnet should be increased from ten or twenty to several hundred. Your batteries can be improved, too. Ten small batteries connected in series produce more voltage than a single large battery.''

''I must admit,'' Morse said, ''that your knowledge of electricity and magnetism is far greater than my own.''

"Not at all," Gale said. "For several years a friend of mine named Joseph Henry has been making new and more powerful batteries and magnets. He teaches at Princeton and spends his spare time making electrical gadgets. He's invented an electric doorbell, and his electromagnets are the strongest in the world."

"I've never even heard of Joseph Henry," Morse admitted.

Professor Gale said, "Henry is a profoundly religious man who enjoys advancing science and discovering new truths. He became interested in electromagnetism in 1827 when he attended a series of lectures by Professor Dana."

"Why, I attended those lectures, too," Samuel said.

"Anyway," Professor Gale said, "Henry published a summary of his discoveries in Silliman's *American Journal of Science* in 1831."

"I was in Europe at the time," Samuel explained.

"In the article, Joseph Henry described the difference in the amount of electricity, or current, and the intensity of electricity, or voltage. Voltage is what you need to transmit electricity over a long wire."

Professor Gale offered to help Samuel Morse. Together they constructed new batteries and added hundreds of turns of wire around the magnets. By November of 1837, Morse and Gale succeeded in sending a message through ten miles of wire coiled on reels.

"Even I am astonished that it works so well," Samuel said.

"Then it's time for a public demonstration," Professor Gale said. "You are not the only one working on an electric telegraph. Other inventors in both America and abroad are working on ideas for sending messages by electricity."

"But none could be anywhere nearly as successful as this one," Samuel said.

"Then exhibit it in public so you can prove to the world that your instrument works," Professor Gale urged.

"I hesitate to show it until it is perfected," Morse said.

Professor Gale said, "What you need is an investment partner, someone with money to buy better materials and hire a skilled mechanic to make the parts. I urge you to make private showings. It's the best way to attract someone to invest in your idea."

Samuel stood in the middle of the room, thoughtfully considering the clutter around him. "You're right," he said at last. "But I want men we can trust. A dishonest person could learn the details of the telegraph and build one of his own. Such an unscrupulous person would use it for his own benefit to line his pockets with money, rather than as a service to mankind, which is what I intend."

Professor Gale agreed. "I'll help you select people who can be depended upon not to disclose the details of your invention."

Together they carefully drew up a list of people to invite to the private showing: Henry B. Tappan, Robert Rankin, Daniel Huntington, Paul Cooper, Commodore Shubrick, and a few others.

The list of names satisfied Samuel. "These men will appreciate the telegraph even in its unfinished form," he predicted.

As the men filed into the laboratory, they exchanged glances, frankly puzzled to see mechanical parts strewn around the artist's apartment.

Samuel described the purpose of the invention.

As he spoke Robert Rankin tapped his temple and winked at the others as if to say here is a brilliant artist who has gone wrong.

Samuel pressed on. "There is no chance for a

mistake in the reading. The telegraph doesn't depend upon sight. Night or day, cloudy or bright, I can still send messages.''

He invited each man to whisper a secret message into his ear. Samuel operated the key. ''Watch the pencil over by Professor Gale.''

The key clicked; the pencil raised and lowered; the paper rolled. Professor Gale tore off the paper and read the dot and dash message.

After sending the last message, Samuel Morse said, ''Tell me, what do you think of it?''

''Well, Professor Morse,'' Robert Rankin said, ''you have a pretty toy. In theory it works. But practically it is useful only as an ornament to decorate a mantel above the fireplace. Or, for the lady of the house to send for the maid in the cellar!''

Paul Cooper disagreed. ''Several years ago another painter proposed a visionary scheme to me and I laughed at his idea. The painter's name was Robert Fulton and his wild idea was a steamboat. I've learned my lesson!''

Samuel waited for more comments. Instead, the men excused themselves and filed out of the room. None of them stayed behind to learn more about the telegraph.

Samuel closed the door as the last man left. ''They didn't even stay to ask questions!'' Samuel said.

The door opened and Alfred Vail, a student, looked in. ''Am I too late for the demonstration?''

''The demonstration is over,'' Samuel said abruptly.

Disappointed, Alfred Vail began to leave.

Although merely a student, and not on their invitation list, Samuel didn't have the heart to let Alfred Vail turn away.

''Wait a moment,'' Samuel said.

Samuel did know a little about Alfred Vail. In fact, they both attended the same church on Mercer Street. Alfred Vail had studied for the ministry, but abandoned that career because of poor health. He'd applied to work in the Philadelphia mint but didn't receive that job. Discouraged, the twenty-nine-year-old student was looking for something to do.

"We'll show the telegraph to you," Samuel Morse said.

As Samuel tapped out the message, Alfred Vail's eyes grew bright with barely controlled excitement. He stayed for hours and asked dozens of questions. Clearly the telegraph impressed him. He left the room in high spirits.

The next day, Alfred Vail again appeared at Samuel's door. "I couldn't sleep at all last night," Alfred Vail said. "After seeing your telegraph, I returned to my boarding-house room, locked the door, threw myself on the bed, and spent all night speculating on what the telegraph could do. I pulled out maps and traced where the important telegraph lines should go.

"But there is one question," Alfred Vail continued. "How far will the current flow before it becomes too weak?"

"Two years ago the same question bothered me, so I devised a relay system." Morse unfolded a sheet of paper with a drawing of the relay. "Before the current becomes too feeble a magnet throws in another set of batteries to boost the message."

Alfred Vail poured over the drawing.

"I'm sure it will work," Samuel Morse told Alfred Vail. "If a message can be sent ten miles, then it can be sent around the world."

"I would like to work with you on the telegraph," Alfred Vail said.

"Well . . ." Samuel began. What could Alfred Vail possibly bring to the project?

"I have no money," Alfred Vail said. "But I am a good mechanic."

"I need a mechanic," Samuel admitted, "but I cannot employ one nor do I have funds to buy materials."

"But it's perfect!" Alfred Vail said. "My father and older brother own and operate the Speedwell Iron Works in Morristown, New Jersey. We make steam engines and other machinery. There's a machine shop I can use. I will have everything I need to make a professional looking instrument."

Samuel Morse agreed to let Alfred Vail construct an improved model of the telegraph.

"We'll make a public test before Washington officials," Samuel said.

"Do you expect to sell the telegraph to the government?" Alfred Vail asked.

"Yes," Samuel said, "to the Post Office Department, I think."

Morse stayed in Morristown, twenty-five miles from New York. He visited the Iron Works during the day. When he was not busy helping Vail, he painted portraits of the family for the fun of it.

"I'm afraid my father has lost faith in our project," Alfred Vail confided in Samuel one day.

"Why?" Samuel asked.

"He approved at first, but when his neighbors learned the details, they sneered at the whole idea."

The two inventors decided to avoid Alfred's father until they could present him with the working model.

Samuel made ready to secure a patent. He wrote to Henry Ellsworth, his Yale classmate. Mr. Ellsworth had become commissioner of patents. In his petition to the Patent Office in Washington, Samuel carefully set forth all of the specifications of the telegraph.

First. The fullest and most precise information can be almost instantaneously transmitted between any two or more points between which a wire conductor is laid.

Second. The same full intelligence can be communicated at any moment, irrespective of the time of day or night, or state of the weather.

Third. The whole apparatus will occupy but little space.

Fourth. The record of intelligence is made in a permanent manner.

Fifth. Communications are secret to all but the persons for whom they are intended.

Morse and Vail examined every part of the telegraph to make it less complex. The pencil marker bothered them the most. Sometimes it jammed; other times it failed to mark clearly.

"Maybe we could get along without a pencil," Alfred suggested. "Telegraph operators will be able to read the message by listening to the click of the metal rod as the electric magnet turns on and off."

"No-o-o," Samuel said slowly. "I've described the instrument as a 'recording' telegraph. It wouldn't be the same without a written record of the dots and dashes."

A few days later Samuel Morse returned from a trip to New York. "Throw away the pencil," Samuel announced. "I've found a replacement for it."

"What do you have?" Alfred Vail asked.

"It's a new invention called a 'fountain pen,' " Samuel said.

They tried the fountain pen and it wrote perfectly.

Finally, on the sixth of January, 1838, they were ready. They proudly invited Judge Vail to come to the workshop and witness the telegraph in operation.

Alfred manned the key, and Samuel stood ready at the receiver near at the entrance to the iron works.

"Have you selected a message?" Alfred asked his father.

"Hummph," the judge said. "Do you really think this contraption will work?"

"We'll see," Alfred said with more confidence than he actually felt.

Judge Vail wrote on a slip of paper. "If you can send this," he said, handing it to Alfred, "and Mr. Morse can read it at the other end, I shall be convinced."

Slowly Vail clicked off the message. They waited in silence.

Samuel burst into the room. He said in triumph, "A patient waiter is no loser!"

Judge Vail's mouth fell open. He jumped up and shook their hands. "That's the message. You must go to Washington at once and urge Congress to build a telegraph line!"

"On to Washington!" Samuel said, his voice filled with triumph. "The instrument is ready for the public."

"I'm certain we'll be successful in Washington, too," Alfred Vail said. He imagined everyone would share his enthusiasm for the telegraph. "We'll only need to show the invention to Congress in order to prove its worth."

"I'll ask Congress for enough money to build a test line," Samuel said.

"How long a line?" Alfred Vail asked.

"One line running from Washington to Baltimore should be a fair test," Samuel decided.

Before they left for Washington, however, Samuel received a letter from the members of the Franklin Institute in Philadelphia. Samuel showed the letter to

Alfred Vail. "Mr. Patterson, the director of the mint in Philadelphia, writes to ask us to demonstrate the telegraph to the Franklin Institute."

"Should we accept his invitation?" Alfred Vail asked. "Congress will adjourn in a few weeks. Time is precious."

"I think it's worth our time," Morse said. "The men belonging to the Franklin Institute are eminent scientists or great master mechanics. It will be the first examination of the telegraph by a scientific body."

The exhibition at the Franklin Institute went without a hitch. Samuel told the members, "Benjamin Franklin discovered the true nature of electricity. The telegraph is the first invention to use electricity for the service of mankind. It is fitting to show it to the institute named in Franklin's honor."

Members of the Franklin Institute wrote a public report praising the telegraph. Six of the greatest men of science in the country signed the report.

Alfred Vail said, "It's time to show the telegraph's powers to the powers that be!"

In Washington, the Committee on Commerce placed a room at Samuel's disposal. There he and his two partners set up the telegraph and connected it to ten miles of wire coiled on giant spools.

Samuel Morse patiently explained the telegraph to all who came: congressmen, men of science, ambassadors from other countries, and businessmen.

"Mr. Dickerson, Secretary of the Navy, will be our most important visitor," Professor Gale said.

"Why?" Alfred Vail asked.

"He'll decide if the president should come for a showing," Professor Gale explained.

With a critical eye, Mr. Dickerson watched the telegraph operate. As he left he said, "I'll recommend that President Van Buren witness the telegraph in

operation tomorrow at one o'clock. Can you be ready?"

"Of course," Samuel Morse said.

The three men tested the equipment and then locked the room. Five years had passed since Samuel sailed the Atlantic on the *Sully* and sketched the idea in his notebook. Now its future came down to a make-or-break test before the president of the United States.

The next afternoon President Van Buren and a company of his aides crowded into the room.

"Well, Mr. Morse," President Van Buren said, "show me what your thunder and lightning jim-crack can do."

The equipment worked flawlessly.

President Van Buren watched without expression. The spark of interest never entered his eyes. The president and his men lacked the burning conviction that they were seeing a revolutionary invention. President

Van Buren thanked Samuel politely and left the three inventors alone in the room.

Samuel Morse, Alfred Vail, and Professor Leonard Gale glumly set about packing the equipment.

"Next year?" Professor Gale asked.

Samuel didn't answer. The president's abrupt dismissal hurt him more than he was willing to admit. He kept looking away and blinking back tears of disappointment.

Five years, Samuel thought. Five years of poverty and unending hardships. "I'm . . . I'm not sure I can endure another year of disappointment," Samuel Morse said at last.

In actual fact, Samuel Morse's endurance had hardly begun to be tested.

10
A Photographic Interlude

Francis O. J. Smith, a shrewd and brisk lawyer from Portland, Maine, presided over the Committee on Commerce. He talked so fast his associates called him 'Fog' Smith.

Fog Smith tried to raise Samuel's sagging spirits. "Congress is a deliberate body and you must give them time to act," Fog Smith said. He tossed his hand to one side in dismissal. "The other congressmen do not understand the powers of electricity the way you and I do."

"The way you do?" Samuel asked. "You've studied electricity?"

"No, of course not. But I do understand its potential," Fog Smith said. "You have a great invention. I have no doubt of its eventual success, given enough time."

Professor Gale spoke. "Having patience is all well and good, but we have no money to play a waiting game."

"You need an assistant to promote the telegraph. You need someone to pilot you through the ins and outs of Washington."

"But who?" Samuel Morse asked.

Fog Smith said, "I offer my own services—provided I become a partner in your enterprise."

After Fog Smith left, the three partners discussed the offer.

"Mr. Smith is without exception the most driving and energetic man I've ever met," Professor Gale said. "We've gone about as far as we can without the help of a legal mind. We need someone who can deal with hard-headed businessmen and suspicious government officials."

"He's a born salesman," Alfred Vail agreed. "I'm willing to reduce my share to have Smith on our team."

Samuel Morse accepted Fog Smith's offer. The four partners divided ownership of the telegraph into sixteen shares. Samuel Morse kept nine shares (a little more than half), Fog Smith got four shares, Alfred Vail got two shares and Professor Gale got one share.

The partners decided that Samuel would sail to England and to France. He would secure the foreign patents and sell the telegraph abroad.

"When he gets back," Fog Smith assured everyone, "the American patent will be granted."

In England, Samuel found two telegraphs in competition with his. Even his old friend Charles Leslie had heard of the competition. "Professor Charles Wheatstone and Mr. William Cooke have a telegraph," Leslie said. "So does Edward Davy."

"Upon what principles do their telegraphs work?" Samuel asked.

"I don't know," Leslie admitted. "Both are called 'needle' telegraphs, whatever that means."

"I'd like to see one," Samuel said.

"Maybe you can," Leslie said. "Davy's telegraph is on exhibit at Exeter house on the Strand."

The tiny room where Davy demonstrated his telegraph did not inspire confidence. Samuel crowded into the dusty room and paid a shilling to see a message being sent.

"Does the telegraph record the message?" Samuel asked the operator.

"No. Not yet," the operator said. "Instead, I watch as electricity causes the compass needle to flip to one side or the other."

The operator seemed to be having problems.

"What's the trouble?" Samuel asked.

"Static electricity interferes occasionally," the operator admitted. "It's only a minor nuisance."

Samuel came out of the small, poorly lighted room with his spirits greatly raised. What he'd seen could not possibly compete with his device.

Next, Samuel studied Wheatstone's telegraph at the Patent Office.

Afterward he met with a group of businessmen to tell them about his telegraph. "Wheatstone's invention is ingenious and beautiful," Samuel said, "but very complicated. On the other hand, Davy's telegraph is crude, unreliable, and doesn't record the message. The slightest amount of static electricity causes the needle to swing wildly from one side to another. My American telegraph is vastly superior to both machines."

The English businessmen did admire the simplicity and reliability of the Morse telegraph. However—

"We can only invest in an instrument with a patent," one of the businessmen explained. "It's the only way to protect against unfair competition."

Samuel said, "I have arranged a meeting with the Attorney General. I'm certain my telegraph is essentially different from the others. A patent will be granted."

But Sir John Campbell, the Attorney General, ignored Samuel's model of the telegraph. Instead, he stated that a London magazine had published an account of the American telegraph.

"According to English law," Sir John Campbell said, "a patent cannot be granted because the details of your invention have been revealed in print."

Samuel protested. "I've published nothing about the telegraph."

"Your application for a patent is denied," Sir Campbell said. He stood in dismissal. "Good day."

Dismayed, Samuel tracked the story about his telegraph to the February 10, 1838, *Mechanics Magazine*. That magazine had simply reprinted the *Morristown Journal* newspaper report of the telegraph tests at the Speedwell Iron Works.

Samuel insisted upon a second hearing. He wrote a long letter in his defense. "The newspaper article doesn't contain enough details to construct a telegraph," he wrote.

While Samuel waited for the second hearing, Charles Leslie arranged for him to attend the coronation of Queen Victoria.

"Everybody will be there," Leslie said, "Ambassadors and princes, pickpockets and beggars."

Charles Leslie and Samuel Morse watched the imposing ceremonies at Westminster Abbey. Queen Victoria, only eighteen years old, seemed lost in the vast hall and the swirl of activity around her.

A few days later, Samuel Morse once again appeared before Sir John Campbell.

Samuel said, "As I explained in my letter, the newspaper article merely described the telegraph in operation. It gave no details concerning its construction."

"I have not read your letter," the Attorney General said. He carelessly flipped through the pages. "Tell me, Mr. Morse, have you taken measures to secure a patent in America?"

"Yes," Samuel said.

"America is large," Sir Campbell replied. "You ought to be satisfied with a patent there."

Once again the Attorney General denied a patent. Samuel could appeal, but only to Parliament. Rather than delaying any longer in England, he sailed to France and began anew there.

Samuel filed for a French patent as soon as he arrived in Paris. Within a few days—and much to his surprise—his lawyer announced the good news.

"A patent has been granted."

"So soon!" Samuel said.

"But—" the lawyer began.

Samuel's face fell. "Always another obstacle!"

The lawyer explained, "By French patent law, your invention must be put to practical use within two years. Otherwise, your patent will be lost."

Thoughtfully, Samuel left the lawyer's office. He walked along rue Neure des Mathurins and up the three flights of stairs to his apartment. He shared it with Reverend Edward N. Kirk of Boston.

Samuel told Reverend Kirk, "I'll need to bring the telegraph to the attention of the public quickly."

"I'll be your interpreter if you wish," Reverend Kirk offered. He spoke French fluently. "I'll make it a point to be home every Tuesday afternoon. You can schedule demonstrations on that day."

Together they laid out the equipment in the small

apartment: the receiver in the parlor, the transmitter in the bedroom, wires and batteries in the hall between.

Francois Arago, director of the Royal Observatory and a fiery political leader, came to their door.

Reverend Kirk recognized the man as he climbed the steps. He urgently whispered to Samuel, "It's Francois Arago! He's the greatest scientist in France, and the guiding hand behind the Academy of Science."

Samuel showed the great man the telegraph in operation.

"Marvelous!" Francois Arago said. He was a well-dressed, confident man. "Will you demonstrate the telegraph before the Academy?"

On the day of the formal presentation, Samuel looked around the lecture hall. As he looked at the greatest gathering of scientists he would ever be likely to meet, stage fright struck. His carefully rehearsed introduction fled from his mind.

Francois Arago saw his distress and immediately took over. Speaking in French, he described the details of the telegraph as Samuel operated it.

A buzz of admiration filled the lecture hall.

"Extraordinaire!"

"Tres admirable!"

Another scientist said, "It is glorious."

Baron Humboldt came forward and warmly greeted Morse. "Your telegraph is the best."

The newspapers in Paris wrote about the American telegraph in the most favorable terms.

A constant stream of visitors climbed the stairs to the apartment to call upon Morse. Businessmen, government officials, and scientists came to marvel at the American telegraph and compliment Samuel upon his success.

But compliments from the visitors would mean little if he failed to interest businessmen in laying a test line.

Samuel pinned his greatest hopes on Monsieur Turneysen, director of the Saint-Germain Railroad Company.

"I am interested in running your telegraph on our railroad from Paris to Saint-Germain, a distance of seven miles," Monsieur Turneysen said. "Can it be done?"

"By all means," Samuel said. "When can we start?"

"Ah, a few details must be worked out first," Monsieur Turneysen said. "I'll call upon you when we are ready."

While Samuel waited, Francois Arago took him to one of the most popular attractions in Paris. "For fifteen years, Louis Daguerre has operated the Diorama, a theater without actors. Each year the show becomes more spectacular."

Louis Daguerre met Samuel Morse and Francois Arago at the door to his theater. He ushered them into the hall for a private showing.

As the lights dimmed, Samuel found himself before a painting of the city of Edinburgh, Scotland. It showed the city by moonlight during a fire. The scene looked so *real*. Flames leaped into the air, and moonlight shimmered on the water.

Louis Daguerre said, "The illusion is created by optical effects—mirrors, transparent paintings, and lights both before and behind the canvas."

A revolving floor carried the three spectators from that incredible sight to the next.

Now they stood at the end of a wide street running into an Alpine village. A mountain of tremendous height, covered with eternal snow, towered over the village.

"I almost want to step onto the stage and climb to the summit of the mountain," Samuel said. "I can hardly believe I am looking at painted canvas."

Francois Arago took a coin and pitched it into the scene. Instead of landing on the street, it struck the canvas and fell to the stage floor. "The canvas is nearer than it appears."

Suddenly an avalanche swept away the Alpine village.

Another scene replaced it. Darkness filled a church, candles were lighted, the faithful came to worship, then the rising sun shone through the stained-glass windows.

"I've never seen anything like this," Samuel said.

Francois Arago said, "Louis Daguerre has something even more amazing to show you."

"What could be more amazing than the Diorama?" Samuel asked.

Louis Daguerre said, "As an artist, I was studying my face reflected in a mirror. I thought how grand it would be if I could invent a mirror with a memory, one that captured the image put before it."

Francois Arago explained, "For years Louis has experimented in making permanent the images of a camera obscura."

Samuel understood. "Professor Silliman and I experimented with photography years ago, but we gave it up as impractical."

"I'll let you judge how impractical it is," Louis Daguerre said. He took Samuel Morse across the city to his workroom. There he allowed Samuel to see the first examples of photography.

The silver-coated sheets of copper showed scenes of Notre Dame Cathedral, a bridge across the Seine, and Paris streets.

In one plate, Samuel could see the tiny letters on a sign. Daguerre gave him a magnifying glass. Through it he could read every letter, tiny but perfectly formed.

"No painting can ever approach the detail visible in your Daguerrotypes," Samuel said. "Have you taken portraits?"

Daguerre said, "No. Even in bright sunlight at noon, an exposure takes ten minutes. Portraits are out of the question because subjects cannot sit still long enough."

Samuel examined a street view. "Look," he said. "Here's a gentleman having his boots polished. The boots and legs are recorded clearly because he held his feet still. Portraits may be possible."

Daguerre disagreed. "But the upper part of the figure is blurred because he moved."

Francois Arago said, "I've urged Louis to make public the details of his process. But so far it is a secret only he possesses."

Daguerre said, "The process is the result of long years of work. It is only fair for my labors to be rewarded."

Samuel could certainly agree with Louis Daguerre. "I know what it means for a person to invest his time and fortune in perfecting an invention."

The next day, Morse invited Daguerre to see the telegraph. At noon on March 8, 1839, Daguerre climbed the three flights of stairs to the apartment.

Daguerre spent an hour examining the telegraph. He said, "I'm delighted with your—"

The clatter of someone running up the stairs interrupted them.

Breathlessly, the messenger cried, "The Diorama is afire!"

Louis Daguerre and Samuel Morse raced across the city. Flames totally engulfed the great building and shot far into the sky. Hot coals rained down.

Samuel pulled Daguerre to safety into a doorway across the street.

The Diorama collapsed.

Daguerre moaned, "The Diorama, my home, camera, and notes! All consumed in flame!"

Samuel said, "You are alive, and the secret of photography is safe with you. But you must publish your valuable research so it is not lost to the world."

When Samuel saw Francois Arago a few days later they discussed the terrible tragedy at the Diorama.

Francois agreed with Samuel. "I think it is vitally important for Daguerre to publish the details of his invention."

"Has he agreed?" Samuel said.

"I think he will," Francois Arago said. "The French Government is well-known for its generosity to men of genius. I'll recommend that he be paid a yearly salary to continue photographic experiments."

"I wish America were as generous," Samuel said with feeling.

Samuel's prospects for success faded day by day. Deals with Russia, Greece, and Egypt all came to nothing. His last hope rested with the Saint-Germain Railroad.

Finally, Monsieur Turneysen came to call.

Samuel asked, "Is your company ready to build the telegraph line?"

"Alas, it is impossible," Monsieur Turneysen said. "I must decline your kind offer to let Saint-Germain build the first telegraph."

"Why?" Samuel asked.

"All telegraph systems must belong to the French Government. They cannot be used for private purposes," Turneysen explained.

Despite the setbacks, Samuel Morse did not become bitter. In a letter to friends in Boston he wrote, "I'm going on, through the kindness of Providence. I am perfectly satisfied that, mysterious as it may seem to me, it has all been ordered in view of my Heavenly Father's guiding hand."

In a letter to his partners, he wrote, "I have done my part. The telegraph is approved in the highest quarters—in England, France and at home."

But the generous praise did not translate into orders for telegraph lines. After almost a year in Europe, Samuel left Paris and sailed home, empty-handed.

11

A Dramatic Gesture

Samuel came home aboard the *Great Western*, the largest and finest ship in the world. Launched only two years earlier, the wooden, paddle-wheel steamer was the first successful ocean-going steamship.

The *Great Western* docked at New York on April 15, 1839. Samuel hoped his partners would be waiting to greet him. He wanted to learn about the progress they'd made at home. Samuel stood at the dock, shifting his travel bag from one hand to the other. No one waited to meet him. For some reason, his partners avoided a reunion. He walked to his room at the University Building overlooking Washington Square.

Ahead of him, the janitor was showing a new student to a room. "You have an artist next door, but his studio has been badly neglected. Cobwebs cover the statues, dust covers the canvases, and sketches have fallen to the floor."

The janitor's voice dropped to a whisper. "He's not been here lately. He seems to be getting rather shiftless."

"How do you mean?" the student asked.

"He is wasting his time over some silly invention, a machine by which he expects to send messages from one place to another."

"Who is the painter?" the student asked.

"Samuel Morse," the janitor said.

The student exclaimed, "He's one of America's best painters! Samuel Morse is president of the National Academy of Design."

The news didn't impress the janitor. "He'd do well to stick to his business," he said with a sneer. "Imagine, sending words by streaks of lightning!"

After Samuel settled into his room, he called upon his brother at the *Observer* office.

"How was the trip home?" Sidney asked.

"Stormy," Samuel said. "But the large size of the *Great Western* made the passage much more pleasant than it would otherwise have been."

"What do your partners report?" Sidney asked.

"Professor Gale, Alfred Vail, and Fog Smith—no one has met with me yet. But the storm did delay me. I missed Professor Gale by a single day. He left for Mississippi on Saturday, and I arrived last night."

"He left no message?" Sidney asked.

"He did leave a letter. He says the country has fallen into hard times. Banks are failing. People are out of work. Students walk the streets like beggars. Is all that correct?"

Sidney nodded. "I'm afraid the economy is bleak. A great depression has fallen across America. People who do have money are unwilling to put it into untried ventures."

"Yes, I suppose so," Samuel said. "I have five miles of wire on a spool. Professor Gale thinks I should loan it to Joseph Henry for his scientific experiments."

"Are you going to give it to him? Sidney asked.

Samuel said, "Yes. Henry has an original mind, and the wire will not stand idle while in his hands."

Sidney brightened. "At least your European tour brought honor to yourself and your invention."

"Seldom has success been so empty," Samuel said. "But I did learn of an important new invention by Louis Daguerre, a method to make permanent the images cast by a camera."

"We've heard tantalizing hints about Daguerre's sun pictures. You must write an article for the *Observer* about it," Sidney insisted. "People are eager to read a first-hand account."

Samuel wrote a letter for Sidney to publish in the New York *Observer*. He told about the wonders of the Diorama and its terrible destruction. In addition he described the daguerreotypes.

Samuel's letter aroused tremendous interest in photography. Newspapers throughout the country reprinted the letter.

Alfred Vail wrote to Samuel and frankly apologized for the lack of progress. "Times are very hard indeed. My father and I will have to forget the telegraph for now. Father says there is no one he'd rather assist than you, if he could. But in the present state of our affairs, we cannot undertake anything more than to pay our bills as they become due, of which there are not a few."

Fog Smith did, finally, meet with Samuel Morse. The man who'd joined because of the prospect of quick profits, now bemoaned the expenses.

"I'm at the end of my rope," Smith said. "I can spend no more time or money on your invention."

"Look at it from my point of view," Samuel said. "I returned with not a coin in my pocket. I have to borrow even for my meals. I am quite disappointed in finding nothing done by Congress."

"I shall be in Washington next winter," Fog Smith promised. "I'll try again then."

"Has the patent been granted?" Samuel pressed.

"No," Fog Smith said. Quickly he added, "But I do expect it to be issued any day now."

Reluctantly, Samuel realized his partners had simply left the battle to him alone. From now on, Samuel would have to rely upon himself, and upon God.

Samuel wrote hundreds of letters telling people about the telegraph and trying to interest them in it. How much easier communication would be with a telegraph! *Dot dash dot dot dot*, instantly his letter would flash to any city in the nation. *Click click click*, instantly he would receive a reply.

He wrote letters asking for help to build a test line, then waited in anxious suspense for replies. Days, weeks, even months would pass before a reply came. The delays became almost unbearable.

He remembered the delay in learning of Lucretia's death.

Lucretia! Fifteen years ago she'd been taken away. Yet Samuel sometimes felt her loss as sharply as if it had occurred the previous day.

The year 1840 marked some progress. On June 20, Samuel received the American patent on his invention. But the news caused hardly a ripple of interest in the telegraph. The letters, when they did arrive, were uniformly lacking in enthusiasm.

Samuel began tutoring again at the University. Although he charged only fifty dollars for three months' study, many students could not afford the payments. Some dropped out. Others fell behind in paying.

He came to the point where he had to choose between buying food or buying postage for his letters.

He took to skipping meals. The near-starvation diet emphasized his hatchet face—long thin nose, deep-set eyes, and hollow cheeks. He began wearing several layers of clothing and bulky coats to hide his painfully thin body.

One day the ache of hunger awoke Samuel. He'd gone for two days without eating. Desperate, he called upon David Strother, one of his students who still owed for his lessons. As Samuel stood outside the door and knocked, his vision blurred, his ears rang, his legs shook. He was at the edge of collapse.

David Strother answered the door. He grabbed Samuel's arm and caught him. "Professor Morse! Are you all right?"

Dazed, Samuel said, "Strother, my boy, how are we off for money?"

David Strother said, "I'm sorry to say I have come up short. I cannot pay until next week."

Samuel shook his head sadly, "Next week! I shall be dead by that time."

"Dead, sir?" David asked.

"Yes, dead by starvation!"

Astonished, David said hurriedly, "Would ten dollars be of any service?"

"Ten dollars would save my life, that's all it would do."

"Then come with me and we will dine together," David Strother said.

The two, teacher and student, enjoyed a modest meal. Samuel declared it to be the best he'd eaten in weeks.

"What is this I hear about Daguerre's sun pictures?" Strother asked. "Are they real?"

"Real enough," Samuel said.

"But if it is true, they'll put artists out of business."

"Not at all," Samuel assured the student.

"Daguerreotypes will only put out of business those who dabble in art. Besides, artists make their money by portraits. According to Daguerre, portraits are impossible. But I think—"

"I'd like to learn about the process," David Strother interrupted.

"Maybe you can," Samuel said. "A few days ago Daguerre made his discovery public. He agreed to tell about it in return for a yearly pension from the French government."

David Strother shook his head. "I've heard his methods are not easy to learn."

"Humm . . . ," Samuel said. "Maybe offering classes in photography would be a way to raise money. But before I can teach others, I'll have to learn how to do it myself."

David Strother asked, "Didn't Daguerre show you how to make daguerreotypes?"

"No, he only showed me the final results."

Daguerre published a pamphlet describing the secrets of his invention. The pamphlet became an international bestseller. Many people eagerly bought it, only to be baffled by the technical language.

Samuel bought Daguerre's pamphlet. The directions were obscure, but Samuel had one advantage. He'd actually held a daguerreotype in his hands. His experience with cameras and chemicals at Yale helped, too.

Samuel set up his camera in the staircase of the University Building. He pointed it out of a third-story window toward the Unitarian Church. An exposure of fifteen minutes produced a successful view of the brick building.

A newspaper reporter saw the photograph. "It is a perfect and beautiful view," the reporter wrote. "It is the first daguerreotype made in this country."

Samuel had taken *one* of the first photographs in America, but he knew he hadn't been first. Samuel didn't want to take credit for something he'd not done. He called upon the reporter to set the record straight. "The specimen I showed you was my first result. The honor of taking the first daguerreotypes in this country belongs to a gentleman named D. W. Seager."

Samuel soon had a partner in his photographic enterprises. John William Draper, a science professor at the University, had taken up photography, too. "I want to capture the images of heavenly bodies, especially the moon," Draper said.

Samuel objected, "The light of the moon is too weak."

"Maybe not," Draper said. "I've built a camera that produces brighter images."

"In that case," Samuel said, "perhaps portraits are possible after all."

The two men decided to work together. At first both Draper and Morse followed Daguerre's directions to the letter. But as they gained experience, they struck out on their own. They built a glass-roofed studio on top of the University building. They made their own cameras, mixed chemicals, and arranged mirrors on the roof to concentrate light upon the sitters.

At last Morse and Draper were ready to try their hand at taking portraits. Samuel's daughter Susan (married now, but still his 'little girl') and some of her friends visited New York. They volunteered to sit before the camera.

Samuel explained, "The iron clamp on the back of each chair keeps your head from moving. The reflectors concentrate sunlight on your face. Take your pose and hold it."

"How long?" Susan asked.

"Oh, ten minutes should be enough," Samuel said.

He uncovered the camera lens, and the exposure began. "Don't move. Look pleasant."

Gallantly the girls tried to hold their pose. The white hot sunlight washed over their faces. Tears came to their eyes. Their complexions tanned under the relentless rays.

Despite the ordeal, the girls stayed motionless. At last Samuel replaced the lens cap. "All right," Samuel said. "You can move now."

"Can we see the picture?" Susan asked.

"As soon as we develop it," Samuel promised.

He took the silver-coated copper plate and put it in a box filled with heated mercury vapor. "Show yourself," Samuel said with a dramatic flare.

The girls watched through a window in the side of the box. They squealed with delight as the image came into view.

"It worked!" Draper said.

Samuel removed the portrait and put it out for all to see.

By summer Samuel Morse and John Draper succeeded in reducing the exposure to only sixty seconds. Young men flocked to the sun studio. They willingly paid in advance the fee of fifty dollars to learn the secrets of taking daguerreotypes.

Samuel Morse became the foremost authority on photography. He trained more students in the art than anyone else during those first years.

One student named Mathew Brady worked as a clerk at Stewart's Dry Goods Store. He was anxious to find a new career to escape from his dead-end job. Mathew Brady enthusiastically embraced photography as his chosen profession. He bubbled over with plans to bring photographs of famous Americans before the public. ''I'm going to start a Hall of Great Americans. Inside will be photographs of generals, presidents, and American heroes.''

''I wish you success,'' Samuel Morse said. But he remembered his own disappointment in trying to present his painting of the House of Representatives to the public.

Mathew Brady said, ''But I'll never be as famous as you, Samuel Morse! People are already calling you the father of American photography.''

Samuel sighed. ''I'd rather be known as the father of the American telegraph.''

In the fall of 1842, Samuel finished an exposure and recorded the time and date in his notebook: October 1, 1842. The first day of October! Ten years ago to the day he'd boarded the *Sully*. Ten years ago he'd gotten the idea for the telegraph.

''I must do something to draw public attention to the telegraph,'' Samuel resolved. ''It must be a dramatic gesture, something to capture the imagination of the public.''

But what? After careful planning he decided to send a message under water across New York Harbor!

He needed two miles of wire. To save money, Samuel bought a strand of copper only a tiny fraction of an inch in diameter. By hand he wrapped the wire with strands of hemp. By hand he insulated it with tar, pitch, and India rubber.

On the evening of October 18, 1842, he carried the reel of wire to a point of land called the Battery at the tip of Manhattan. There he hired a man with a small rowboat.

While the man rowed, Samuel sat at the stern and paid out the homemade wire cable.

During the beautiful moonlight night, men and women strolling arm in arm along the Battery stopped to watch. They wondered what sort of catch the men in the rowboat could be fishing for, and why they needed such a long line.

After two hours, Morse finished the job. The small cable connected a building, called Castle Garden, at the tip of Manhattan to Governor's Island in the bay.

The next morning the New York *Herald* carried Samuel's announcement. Instead of showing the telegraph to a selected few, Samuel invited the public to see the telegraph in operation.

Early that morning when Samuel arrived at Castle Garden, a crowd of curious on-lookers had already gathered.

Professor Gale, working with Morse again, shook hands with Samuel and took a boat across to Governor's Island.

A few minutes later the receiver clicked. "Professor Gale is at the other end," Samuel explained. "We are ready to test the cable. I will send several letters of the alphabet to Professor Gale, and he will repeat each one back to me."

He seated himself before the instrument. Confidently he clicked out a test message.

The crowd grew silent.

The receiver clicked again, the paper reeled off the reply.

In mid-sentence the receiver stopped.

Samuel tried again. Nothing. He tried again and again.

The line remained dead.

The crowd began to jeer. Someone gave a cat-call.

Swiftly, Samuel examined the apparatus. "I . . . I can't find anything wrong." He stopped in confusion. He sat helplessly before the silent receiver.

A woman giggled.

"Hoax!" one man yelled.

Then Samuel spotted the trouble. A ship had raised anchor and caught the line. Sailors hauled in about two hundred feet of it.

"Stop!" Samuel shouted. Frantically, he waved to attract their attention. They cut the cable and sailed away.

Samuel tried to explain that the line had been cut. The crowd ignored his explanation. Disappointed and irritated at being denied the promised marvel, they drifted away.

Samuel slumped into the chair by his telegraph, dejected.

The dramatic gesture designed to impress the public had turned into a miserable failure.

12

Trouble on the Line

Shortly after the underwater disaster, Joseph Henry, one of the men Samuel respected most, came to visit.

"The time is ripe for your invention," Joseph Henry assured him. "Others have attempted to make a telegraph, but I prefer yours."

During the four years beginning in 1838, Samuel had received encouragement from only one person—Joseph Henry, a fellow Christian. The kind words had kept Samuel Morse going.

Encouraged by Joseph Henry, he wrote an exhaustive letter to C. G. Ferris of New York, the new Chairman of the Committee on Commerce. In clear and cool logic, Samuel set forth the full particulars of his invention. The letter ran to dozens of pages.

Congressman Ferris took an interest in the telegraph. He invited Samuel Morse to Washington to show the telegraph to members of Congress once again. "It is indispensable to give your personal attention to the business."

Samuel wrote to his partners, "I have looked for private investors and found none. The best hope lies with the Congress. But someone must be in Washington to show the telegraph in operation and speak on its behalf." He asked for their help. He needed an assistant to operate the second telegraph station.

But Professor Gale couldn't go. He'd taken a teaching position at a college in Mississippi. Alfred Vail couldn't be spared from his father's business. Fog Smith had written off the entire project as a failure, and he refused to be bothered with it.

Without the help of his partners, Samuel trained James C. Fisher as an assistant. Fisher had come to New York to fill a temporary teaching position at the University.

In December, 1842, Samuel packed his bags and withdrew all of his savings—seven hundred dollars. He set out for Washington once again in a desperate attempt to obtain government backing for the telegraph.

In Washington, Ferris gave him the use of a room held by the House Committee on Commerce. The second telegraph station would be across the Capitol Building in a room belonging to the Senate Committee on Naval Affairs.

In order to string wire between the two stations, Samuel descended into the vast and unused sub-basement. A workman carried a lamp. They came to a dark and dusty chamber where broken tools and old furniture had been stored and forgotten.

The workman stood outside the storeroom. Samuel stepped inside. A ray of light fell upon a ghostly white figure. Samuel drew in his breath, momentarily startled at the frightening, twisted appearance.

Then he peered more closely, hardly believing what

he saw. Samuel rubbed his eyes. He looked once, twice, a third time. Could it be? After all these years—the *Dying Hercules* statue!

Gently he picked it up. The *Dying Hercules* had won for him the Adelphi medal so many years before in London. His own copy had been accidentally thrown away. He'd traced down the others, only to find they'd been destroyed or lost in one way or another.

How long had the statue patiently waited for him? Did it prophesy victory? Or did it foretell defeat? He recalled his own words about the statue. ''Maybe it takes more courage to face defeat than to win a victory.''

Others would have viewed the mysterious presence of the statue and speculated upon what it meant. However, Samuel F. B. Morse never let superstition rule his life. He simply rejoiced at finding the long-lost statue. Then he continued to string the wire.

Later he solved the mystery of how the statue had come to be in the Capitol building basement. He'd given it to Charles Bulfinch, the Capitol architect, who'd stored it in the room and forgotten about it.

That night Congressman John P. Kennedy came to watch as Samuel tested the line. Kennedy said, ''We have the bill ready to introduce, just as soon as your demonstration has convinced them.''

Samuel's natural talents—his dramatic flare, outward appearance of confidence, and ability to speak to strangers—did sway a few doubters. Millard Fillmore, a leader in the House, watched the amazing invention.

''I believe it might succeed,'' Fillmore said. ''You can count on my support.''

Samuel talked to a large number of congressmen. He quoted Joseph Henry and Francois Arago. Both agreed that his telegraph worked best.

Benjamin Silliman helped, too. He published an open letter to Samuel in the *National Intelligencer*, a morning newspaper read by most congressmen. Silliman wrote, "If I have weight enough to carry only one wavering vote, it may be the very one that will cast the decision in your favor."

After the demonstration, came the long waiting to see the bill move out of committee and toward congressional action. It would have to pass both the House and Senate. Samuel waited through December, then January, and into February.

The bill came up before the House of Representatives first. Millard Fillmore engineered the floor debate so that John P. Kennedy could introduce the telegraph bill.

As Samuel watched from the gallery, the clerk read the resolution: ". . . that a sum of thirty thousand dollars be appropriated for testing the usefulness of the electromagnetic telegraph."

Cave Johnson, the representative from Tennessee rose to his feet. "Mr. Speaker, since Congress is doing so much to encourage science, I do not wish to see the science of mesmerism overlooked." He proposed that half of the telegraph money go toward the study of mesmerism (hypnotism).

Mr. Stanley of North Carolina replied, "I have no objection to including mesmerism provided the gentleman from Tennessee is the subject of the experiment."

Cave Johnson laughed and answered, "I have no objection provided Mr. Stanley is the operator."

The hall roared with laughter.

Samuel leaned tensely against the gallery railing. He could not believe the scene before him. The congressmen bantered back and forth as if nothing of importance waited before them. Their jokes threatened to kill his invention by ridicule.

A reporter approached. Samuel Morse waved him away. "I have an awful headache," Samuel told him. He put his hand to his forehead.

"You look anxious," the reporter observed.

"I have reason to be. If you knew how important this is to me, you would not wonder. If it succeeds, I am a made man. If it fails, I am ruined."

The House decided to take up the bill later.

Fretfully, Samuel visited with his Yale classmate, Henry Ellsworth, the Commissioner of Patents. "I am kept in suspense, which is becoming more and more tantalizing and painful. I endeavor to exercise patience."

Henry Ellsworth quoted the Bible passage, " 'Thy will be done.' "

"It is easier to quote it than feel it," Samuel said. "But God knows me better than I know myself. I shall therefore be sustained in all events."

How did Morse appear to others? Horatio Greenough, the sculptor, was in Washington at the time. He wrote to a friend, "Poor Morse is here with his beautiful, his magical telegraph. He goes regularly to the House."

Another man told about seeing Morse. "He has been all winter at Washington trying to push his 'dunder and blixen' telegraph through Congress. I am afraid Uncle Sam will be found to be lightning proof in his case."

After three days, Congressman Kennedy again presented the bill. The debate grew sharp. A large number of congressmen left the chamber. They wanted to avoid voting upon a machine they did not understand.

Morse waited at the back of the hall while the congressmen cast their votes. He tried to keep score, but the figures danced before his eyes. His hands shook too hard to tally the score.

"What's the vote?" Samuel asked under his breath.

"The telegraph bill passed," a man nearby said, "by a margin of 89 to 83."

Seventy congressmen chose not to vote. Other congressmen admitted they voted for the bill, not because they believed in the telegraph, but because they knew and trusted Samuel Morse.

The bill had yet to pass the Senate. In only eight days congress would adjourn. Bills jammed the calendar. Not only might the Senate defeat his bill if it came up for debate, but the Senate might not even take it up before adjourning.

Every morning Samuel walked to the Senate chamber. All day he sat in the gallery and listened to the senators debate the remaining bills. Day after day passed, but his bill did not come up. Every night as the gavel closed the session, Samuel sadly reflected that his bill waited far down on the list.

Then came the last day of the session, March 3. A hundred and forty bills waited ahead of his. The Senate decided to debate until midnight. The president left the White House and waited in a room provided for him at the Capitol, ready to sign the bills passed during the final hurried hours.

Morse sat in the gallery and watched anxiously.

The time grew late. Lamps were lighted. Ten o'clock struck.

Only two hours remained before final adjournment. Yet, a hundred and twenty of the hundred and forty bills remained for consideration. Could his bill be reached before the closing hour?

Samuel consulted with Senator Silas Wright of New York.

"Prepare for the final disappointment," Senator Wright said.

Senator Huntington of Connecticut agreed. "There is no hope that the telegraph bill can be reached before the hour of adjournment."

Senator Wright put a kindly hand on Samuel's shoulder. "There is no use for you to stay here."

Morse had been in the gallery all day. The suspense had stretched his nerves to the breaking point. He could not bear the final blow of hearing the gavel fall to close the session with his telegraph bill unpassed.

With a heavy heart he left the Senate and walked to his hotel. "Should I give it up?" Samuel wondered. "Should I return home, take up painting or photography, and think no more about the telegraph?"

Alone in his room he counted his money. After paying his hotel bill and buying a train ticket home, he would have thirty-seven cents left.

He kneeled down, opened his heart to God, and committed all his affairs to Him. He had done all he could to succeed. Then he lay down and slept the untroubled sleep of a child.

In the morning, as he ate breakfast, a waiter came to his table. "A young lady wishes to speak with you," the waiter said.

"Invite her to my table," Samuel Morse instructed. Actually, he didn't feel like talking to anyone.

Miss Annie G. Ellsworth, the beautiful daughter of the Commissioner of Patents, approached his table. She flashed a warm and bright smile.

"What brings you to see me so early?" Samuel asked. He could not match her happy mood.

"I have come to congratulate you," she said.

"Indeed. For what?"

"On the passage of your bill."

"Oh, no, my young friend, you are mistaken. I was in the Senate chamber until after the lamps were lighted, and my senatorial friends assured me there was no chance for me."

"But," she replied, "it is you that are mistaken. Father stayed until adjournment at midnight. The bill passed without debate. He saw the president put his name to your bill. I asked father if I might come and tell you, and he gave me leave. Am I the first to tell you?"

Morse could not speak. Could it be? Had he won the twelve-year-old battle to give the nation a practical electromagnetic telegraph?

"Yes, Annie," he said at last, "you are the first to inform me. Now I am going to make you a promise. The first dispatch on the completed line from Washington to Baltimore shall be yours."

"I will hold you to your promise," she smiled.

Samuel triumphantly arranged for the construction of the line. He wrote to Alfred Vail, "My news, although short, is sweet. You will be glad to learn that my bill has passed the Senate without opposition."

Samuel enjoyed word games and puns. He couldn't resist one now. "I want to *A. Vail* myself of your services." He placed Alfred Vail in charge of making relays, batteries and the telegraph instruments.

The Mississippi college where Leonard Gale taught had closed, so Gale could join the telegraph operation as scientific advisor.

Both Leonard Gale and Alfred Vail favored laying the line underground. Morse agreed. "It will be safer in the ground and out of the way." The Baltimore & Ohio Railroad gave them permission to use its right-of-way.

The final design called for insulated copper wire to be inserted in lead tubes and buried in the soil. Samuel Morse sent James Fisher, the university teacher, to the factory to oversee the making of the underground cable and to test it for defects.

Fog Smith, as a full partner in the telegraph, insisted he be given a part of the government contract. He became general contractor in charge of laying the cable and immediately came up with a scheme to milk the project for more money. "Since the government is furnishing the funds," Fog Smith said, "the cable-laying contract can be padded to turn a nice profit."

Samuel Morse, shocked, viewed Smith's suggestion with troubled eyes. He hotly denounced using the telegraph for dishonest gain.

Fog Smith did bring one prize to the operation—a Yankee genius named Ezra Cornell. He was a man of unusual practical ability and sound common sense who solved their last remaining problem. He invented a sort of plow to lay the leaden tubes underground.

By October, 1843, all of the necessary planning had been completed. Under the strong, stern hand of Ezra Cornell the actual construction began. His ingenious machine cut a trench, drew the lead pipe from the reel, buried it and covered it, all in a single, swift operation.

By December, Cornell and his crew had laid seven miles of the cable.

Samuel Morse tested the line by sending messages to Alfred Vail.

"What do you say, Mr. Morse?" Ezra Cornell asked. "Is the line all right?"

"No, Mr. Cornell," Samuel replied. "Everything worked well today for a time, but now the signal is not clear. Something is wrong."

At first Samuel thought Alfred Vail had grown rusty at operating the telegraph key. He urged Vail to take more care in forming the letters. "Make a longer space between each letter and a still longer space between each word."

But the problem couldn't be blamed upon Alfred Vail. Every time they tied in another mile of cable, the signal grew less dependable. The telegraph didn't work right. Samuel's own notes told the story: Received signal, but not clear. Sent a message. No answer. Feeble signal.

Samuel checked the key and receiver, the batteries and relays. They worked perfectly.

He held a meeting with Ezra Cornell. "The problem has to be with the cable," Samuel said. "Perhaps the plow damages the cable as it is being laid."

The big, quiet man disagreed. "There be nothing wrong with the plow. Here is where your troubles lie."

He showed Samuel a short length of the cable. With a knife, Ezra Cornell peeled back the lead covering, sliced through the insulation, and laid it open to the wire.

"Why, the insulation has melted," Samuel said. "The copper wire is shorting out against the lead pipe!"

"Yes, Mr. Morse," Ezra said. "The rest of it is just as bad. We've laid seven miles of worthless wire."

"But Fog Smith and James Fisher were supposed to check the wire at the factory."

Ezra Cornell could only shrug. "Someone has not been doing his job."

Samuel said, "I realize now I made a grave error to go underground."

"What do you propose to do?" Ezra Cornell asked.

"I need time to think of a way out of this," Samuel said. "But I don't dare admit publicly that anything is wrong. At the first hint of trouble, Cave Johnson and a dozen other congressmen will be ready to call for an end to the experiment."

Ezra Cornell understood. "I can manage to cause an innocent delay." He grasped the handles of the plow that a team of eight mules drew.

"Hurrah, boys! We must lay another length of pipe before we quit!"

The teamsters cracked their whips over the mules. The animals started off at a lively pace. Cornell tilted the plow handle. He caught the blade on the point of a rock. The plow shattered.

The telegraph crews shut down the operation while Ezra Cornell repaired the plow.

Samuel called his associates together for a council of war. "More than half of the government money has been spent on a line of only seven miles. We have miles and miles of worthless wire stored in the cellar of the Patent Office."

"What can be done?" Alfred Vail asked.

"I don't know—yet," Samuel admitted. "But I am compelled to stop any further trenching until a solution is found."

Fog Smith said, "Why not finish the line anyway?"

"But it doesn't work."

"We'll draw our government salary, nevertheless," Fog Smith pointed out.

Samuel shook his head, furious at a person who valued money above doing what was right.

Samuel couldn't dismiss Fog Smith since he was a partner, but he could put Ezra Cornell in charge of the day-to-day work on the line. Samuel did let James Fisher go, as he'd proven to be unreliable.

But what would Samuel do? How could he finish the line?

13

What Hath God Wrought

Ezra Cornell's broken plow and the onset of winter weather gave Samuel time to look at the telegraph with fresh eyes. He spent the winter in the home of Henry Ellsworth in Washington.

Samuel candidly admitted the true story about the telegraph to his host. "I have never been in more need of prayers," Samuel said. "We spent twenty-three thousand dollars on the worthless line. Fog Smith's greed embarrasses me. Where I expected to find a *friend*, I found a *fiend*. I pray to God for the right spirit in dealing with him."

Merely thinking about Fog Smith's smug unconcern caused Samuel's fingers to tighten. His voice became firm. "I will not let the lost time and lost money defeat the telegraph. The line will be finished, and finished within our budget."

"How can you possibly build a line from Washington to Baltimore with only seven thousand dollars?" Henry Ellsworth asked.

"We hope to recover some of the money," Samuel said. "Ezra Cornell discovered how to extract the wire from the defective pipe. He'll spend the winter cutting the wire out and stripping it of insulation. The wire will be wound upon reels to be used again. The lead will be melted down and sold as scrap.

"Alfred Vail will spend his time in the Library of Congress reading all he can find about European telegraphs."

While Alfred Vail researched European designs, Samuel Morse read through his own notes. "The telegraph has worked from the very beginning," he repeated to himself, drawing comfort from that thought.

One morning in February of 1844, Alfred Vail appeared at Samuel's temporary office in the basement of the Capitol Building.

"Look at this!" Alfred Vail said. He thrust an English journal before Samuel's startled eyes.

"What have you found?" Samuel asked. He rubbed his eyes, weary from the hours of study.

Alfred Vail explained, "According to this article, Wheatstone and Cooke tried an underground cable. It never worked to their satisfaction. Telegraph lines between cities in Europe have all failed because they used underground cables."

"Then an underground line is out," Samuel decided.

"What shall we use instead?" Alfred Vail asked.

"This may be the answer," Samuel said. He tapped his notebook. "This is the notebook I carried aboard the *Sully*."

Alfred Vail came around the table so he could see the sketch. "Posts? You think we can string the wire along the top of tall posts?"

"It would certainly be less expensive," Samuel said. "Strong poles about thirty feet tall, well buried in the ground, and placed two hundred feet apart, can carry the wire.''

Alfred Vail said, ''Insulation will only be needed where the wires touch the poles.''

''Let's talk it over with Mr. Cornell,'' Samuel Morse decided.

They tramped out to Ezra Cornell's workshop in the basement of the Patent Office. The thrifty Cornell had even pulled up the lead pipe already in the ground and salvaged it. In all, he recovered eight thousand dollars worth of materials.

After much discussion, the three men agreed to go with the new design.

Samuel made a swift calculation. ''We'll need a total of seven hundred poles. I'll advertise for them in the local newspapers.''

''Then we're set,'' Alfred Vail said. He felt much better.

''Not entirely,'' Samuel said. ''How shall we insulate the overhead wires where they fasten to the poles? We haven't time to make special insulators. Whatever we use must be easily installed and completely foolproof. We cannot afford a second setback.''

''I'll work on it,'' Alfred Vail promised.

In less than a week, Alfred Vail turned in a model of an insulator.

The practical mind of Ezra Cornell came up with an idea of his own. Ezra Cornell said, ''I believe glass knobs like those used on chest-of-drawers will work.''

Samuel did not dismiss Ezra Cornell's idea out of hand, although he did lean toward Vail's design. But this time Samuel took no chances. He traveled to Princeton, New Jersey. There he held a confidential meeting with Joseph Henry.

A week later Samuel Morse came back from his meeting with Joseph Henry. He went to the workshop where Ezra Cornell worked.

"You're absolutely right," Samuel said. "The glass knobs will make perfect insulators."

"How is that, Mr. Morse? I thought you had decided to use Mr. Vail's plan."

"Yes, I did," Samuel admitted. "But I explained to Joseph Henry the failure of the insulation in the pipes and explained our decision to place the wires on poles in the air. I showed him the model of Mr. Vail's insulator. 'It will not do,' Henry said. Then I explained to him your plan, which he said was the answer."

With the coming of spring, outdoor work resumed. This time Samuel resolved to supervise personally the joining of each section of line and test it all along the way.

Henry Ellsworth and his family held a special dinner in Samuel's honor as construction began.

Samuel presented his host family with a gift—a book on etiquette for Annie Ellsworth.

"How do you manage to be so happy when so many problems press about you?" Annie Ellsworth asked.

Samuel said, "In traveling in Europe some years ago, I saw a sundial. The inscription on it said, 'I note not the hours except they be bright.' "

"What a wonderful idea," Annie said.

"I placed the quotation in my notebook," Samuel said, "and expanded it into a poem."

"Do you recall the poem?" Annie asked.

"I'll write it out for you," Samuel said. He wrote down the two verses of his poem. He gave the sheet to the young woman:

The Sundial

The sun when it shines in the clear cloudless sky
Marks the time on my disk in figures of light.
If clouds gather o'er me, unheeded they fly;
I note not the hours except they be bright.

So when I review all the scenes that have passed
Between me and thee, be they dark, be they light,
I forget what was dark, the light I hold fast;
I note not the hours except they be bright.
—To A. G. E. from S. F. B. M.

The next morning, Morse cheerfully watched the workmen drilling holes along the railroad tracks. They set the poles in place. People stopped to stare at the construction. The line of poles made a stark pattern against the sky, unlike anything ever seen before. The American landscape had been changed forever.

Ezra Cornell said, "Soon every railroad will carry a line of telegraph poles across the horizon."

"So you believe in its success," Samuel said.

"Yes, Mr. Morse. Once you have shown what your invention can do, telegraph lines will crisscross America. I've already told my son-in-law to start learning the Morse code so he can be a telegraph operator. It will become a profession very much in demand."

The work went much faster now that poles were being used. By the middle of April the line ran six miles from Washington.

A reporter from the *Intelligencer* came out for an on-the-spot interview.

"The telegraph helps in its own construction," Samuel told the reporter. "Questions asked at one end of the line can be instantly answered from the other end. I've grown so accustomed to telegraphing my assistants, I sometimes forget and start to speak to them aloud."

"But who would want to use a telegraph?" the reporter asked.

Samuel said, "Someday you'll send your news dispatches by wire rather than sending them on the train."

The reporter found that idea difficult to believe. "But I do hope you're right. I have to cover the Whig and Democrat conventions in Baltimore this spring. It will mean long, boring train rides between Washington and Baltimore."

In May, the nation's two major political parties would hold their conventions to choose candidates to run for president. Samuel realized the conventions presented him with an unexpected opportunity to demonstrate the speed of the telegraph.

He explained to his partners. "Washington residents will be anxious to learn who has been nominated to run for president. If we can get the news to them first, it will give the telegraph a big boost."

Ezra Cornell said, "But we cannot be in Baltimore by convention day."

"We can reach Annapolis Junction where the train stops," Samuel said. "We'll relay the news from there."

Morse, Vail, and Cornell worked overtime to string the telegraph as far as Annapolis Junction by the first of May.

Morse gave his instruction to Alfred Vail. "The train from Baltimore will stop at Annapolis Junction to discharge passengers. Have everything ready. Watch for the train. When it comes into sight from Baltimore, send me a message. I'll be standing by in Washington."

"And then?" Alfred Vail asked.

"Question the passengers to learn who the Whigs nominated for president. Telegraph the information to me."

On convention day, Samuel waited beside the telegraph in the Capitol. At three-thirty in the afternoon he received Alfred Vail's signal.

"The train has come into sight," Samuel told the congressmen who waited.

A moment later the telegraph began a burst of clicks. He read the full dispatch as it arrived.

"The ticket is Henry Clay!"

It became the first telegraphic news flash.

The news circulated throughout Washington. An hour later the train from Baltimore arrived at the capitol. The reporter from the *Intelligencer* jumped from the train, ready to announce the important news.

Instead, a crowd of Clay's supporters greeted the astonished newspaperman. "Hurrah for Clay!" they shouted.

The reporter wrote about both the convention and the amazing telegraph. "In a race between the telegraph line and the railroad line, Mr. Morse's lightning line won."

Construction on the line could not have been going more smoothly. "We'll be into Baltimore within two weeks," Ezra Cornell promised.

Samuel set the date for the official demonstration of the telegraph: Friday, May 24, 1844. As promised, Ezra Cornell completed the entire test line of forty-one miles within the time limit.

Samuel Morse moved the telegraph from the basement room and installed it in the Chamber of the Supreme Court. He invited congressmen, distinguished government officials, and personal friends to witness the first telegraph in the world to send messages between two cities.

On the critical test day, Samuel waited patiently for everyone to gather in the Supreme Court Chamber. He looked over the crowd, amused by the range of emotions before him: doubt in the eyes of Cave Johnson, who'd opposed the telegraph; anxiety on the face of Senator Silas Wright, who'd voted for it; faith expressed by Annie Ellsworth, who'd been the first to tell Samuel about the passage of the telegraph bill.

At nine-forty-five, Samuel Finley Breese Morse stood and faced his audience. "The telegraph line between Washington and Baltimore, Maryland, is complete. My associate Alfred Vail waits at the other end in the Mount Clair train station.

"At my invitation Miss Annie Ellsworth has selected the first official message, the words of which I have not seen. I will transmit the message to Baltimore. As soon as Mr. Vail receives the message, he will send it back to me. It will be recorded on paper both here and in Baltimore."

To Annie he said, "May I have the message?"

Demurely she stepped forward and pressed the slip of paper into his hand.

Samuel read the paper. "What hath God wrought." He, of course, recognized it as a quotation

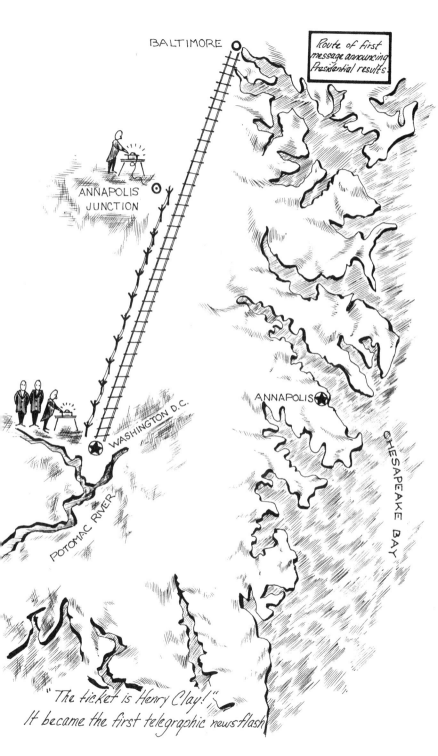

BALTIMORE

Route of first message announcing Presidential results.

ANNAPOLIS JUNCTION

WASHINGTON D.C.

ANNAPOLIS

POTOMAC RIVER

CHESAPEAKE BAY

"The ticket is Henry Clay!"
It became the first telegraphic newsflash

from Holy Scripture, from Numbers 23:23 in the Old Testament. He could not have been more pleased with her choice.

He took his seat before the telegraph.

Calmly he tapped out the message.

The electric current instantly raced to Alfred Vail in Baltimore. Vail immediately echoed it back. The receiver beside Samuel clattered into action. Dots and dashes printed out on the paper roll. Samuel penciled in the letters below the Morse code.

•--	••••	•-	-	••••	•-	-	••••
W	h	a	t	h	a	t	h

--•	••	-••	•--	•	••	••-	--•	••••	-
G	O	D	W	r	o	u	g	h	t

Samuel stood and again faced the audience. In triumph he tore off the ribbon of paper and smoothed it out for all to see.

Their applause washed over him. His face glowed with pleasure. Suddenly, like a dam breaking, the dignified group broke into whoops and hollers. They gathered around to congratulate the inventor and slap him on the back.

Cave Johnson stepped forward and shook Samuel's hand. "Sir, I give in. It is an astonishing invention."

For Samuel Morse the demonstration successfully concluded twelve years of trying. The fickle 'hare' of Andover Academy had set an example of steadfast endurance unmatched in the history of American invention.

What did Samuel Morse think of his invention?

He said, "That sentence of Annie Ellsworth's was divinely inspired, for it will be in my thoughts day and night. 'What had God wrought!' It is His work, and He alone carried me thus far through all my trials and enabled me to triumph over the obstacles, physical and moral, which opposed me.

'' 'Not unto us, not unto us, but to thy name, O Lord, be all the praise.' ''

14
Lightning Line Doctor

Only a few days later the telegraph proved its worth in a practical way. During the Democratic convention, politicians in Baltimore carried on a long-distance debate urging Silas Wright in Washington to accept the nomination to run for vice-president.

More importantly, a family in Washington received word that a family member in Baltimore had died at the convention. Several hours would have passed before the rumor could be confirmed or denied.

By telegraph Samuel asked for Vail to report the true story. In less than ten minutes Alfred Vail found the gentleman in question to be very much alive. The good news set the family's minds at rest.

On another occasion a businessman in Baltimore accepted a check drawn on the Bank of Washington. He did so only after confirming by telegraph that the man who had written the check did, indeed, have enough money in his bank account to cover the amount of the check.

The telegraph changed the world in a fundamental

way. Families could quickly learn of the safe arrival of loved ones at far away destinations. Businessmen could easily control far-flung enterprises.

Within two years, telegraph wires stretched as far north as Portland, Maine, and west to Milwaukee. Investors saw the possibilities. They established the Western Union Telegraph Company. Railroads found the telegraph especially useful to report track conditions and prevent accidents.

For the first time, a communication network could rapidly collect weather information. Weather forecasts became much more reliable.

The telegraph began to earn money for its inventor. The first money he actually received—forty-five dollars—came for a short line between the Post Office and the National Observatory in Washington.

How should he spend his first earnings? Samuel gave it to a church in Washington so the congregation could begin a Sunday school.

Within a few years, the value of the telegraph grew to astronomical sums. A few thousand dollars invested at the beginning became worth millions of dollars.

Such a large amount of money attracted unscrupulous people who tried to claim credit for the telegraph. Others simply wanted to overthrow Morse's patent. In that way, they could build telegraphs without paying Morse for his efforts. In all, more than sixty-two people came forward with one claim or another.

Samuel never claimed more than he deserved. He agreed to the importance of the contributions made by Joseph Henry. ''To Professor Henry is unquestionably due the honor of discovering a fact in science which proved the practicability of exciting magnetism at a distance.

''On the other hand, I claim to be the first to use

electromagnetism for telegraphic purposes, and the first to construct a telegraph."

Eventually, the claims reached the Supreme Court for a final decision. The justices decided in favor of Morse. "Morse alone, in 1837, seems to have reached the most perfect result desirable for public and practical use. The telegraph never was invented, perfected, or put into practical use, until it was done by Morse."

But what about the help given to Morse by Dana, Henry, and others? "The fact that Morse sought and obtained the necessary information from the best sources, and acted upon it, neither impairs his rights as an inventor, nor detracts from his merits."

The opinion of the Supreme Court silenced the critics. Samuel never doubted the outcome. "I read in my Bible, 'The triumph of the wicked is short.'"

In the eyes of the public, and in the eyes of the law, only one person deserved credit for the telegraph— Samuel F. B. Morse. Honors showered upon him from all sides.

For instance, Yale conferred upon him an honorary doctor's degree. The letters of the degree, L.L.D., stood for Latin words meaning doctor of letters. Playfully, Samuel always insisted the letters stood for "Lightning Line Doctor."

Samuel gratefully accepted the honors. Just as gratefully he realized the steady income would let him at last afford a home of his own. He talked it over with his brother Sidney. "For all of these years I've lived in rented apartments or hotel rooms."

Sidney agreed to search for an appropriate estate. He finally pointed Samuel to a hundred-acre property about two miles from Poughkeepsie, New York.

"It's called Locust Grove," Sidney said.

The two brothers visited the place. From the house Morse could see over trees and distant woods down to the water of the Hudson River.

"In that direction," Sidney said and pointed to the north beyond the river, "on a clear day you can see the Catskill Mountains. Poughkeepsie is only two miles away through the woods. It has good markets and schools."

Samuel smiled. "Of what use are schools to me now? All of my children are grown and have homes of their own."

"Well, Poughkeepsie has good churches, too," Sidney said.

"It's perfect," Samuel decided. He bought the property. For the first time in twenty years he and his three children came together under his roof. Samuel's greatest delight was from his grandson— little Charles, Susan's son.

But she could stay at Locust Grove for only a few weeks. Then she and little Charles returned to her husband's plantation in Puerto Rico. His sons left, too.

Samuel stayed alone in the big farmhouse. In the vast, silent building the sense of loneliness became more acute.

For several years Samuel had been attracted to a lovely deaf woman named Sarah Griswold. She first came to his notice during the photograph session when he and Draper struggled to make daguerreotype portraits of Susan and her friends. Sarah Griswold was one of Susan's friends.

At the time, Samuel put the thought of marriage out of his mind. He was penniless and could not begin a second family. He kept his feelings about Sarah to himself. Someday the telegraph will be successful, he told himself. Someday he'd own a home of his own. When he did, he'd ask Sarah to marry him.

Now, with his fame and fortune assured, he waited no longer. He proposed marriage to Sarah, and she agreed.

Sarah bore him one daughter, Leila, and three sons, William, Arthur, and Edward. "Sweet Eddie" was the youngest and the one who grew up to be the most like his father.

As the family grew, Samuel completely rebuilt Locust Grove in the style of an elaborate Italian villa.

He spent most of the morning in the study, reading, writing, and listening to the sound of his children playing.

For exercise he would go exploring with them through the glens, brooks, and forests all around. Along the way they would pause to listen to birds sing, or stop to pick wild flowers.

Samuel loved animals. A little flying squirrel became so fond of Samuel it would sit on his shoulder and beg for food. Morse took the delightful little animal with him wherever he went, even on a trip to New York. The flying squirrel behaved itself properly. It slept in Samuel's coat pocket and ate from his hands.

For more than a quarter century Samuel spent his days as a country gentleman. The life at Locust Grove suited him perfectly.

Benson Lossing, a historian and one of his neighbors, asked a question. "You spent so many years in New York and Washington. How can you bury yourself in the country so far from your friends and business associates?"

"Come into the study," Samuel invited. "I'll show you how it is possible."

He escorted Benson Lossing into the study and pointed to a telegraph on a small table beside his desk.

"Here is how I stay in touch," Samuel said. "A private telegraph line connects my study to the outside world. With only a touch of the key I can communicate instantly to anyone in the nation—or even across the ocean by Cyrus Field's Atlantic cable."

A unique bond had grown up between Samuel Morse and the telegraph operators and messengers. They called themselves a telegraph "family." Morse called the multitude of mostly young telegraphers and messengers his "children."

Early in 1870 his "children" began to plan for a special celebration. Robert B. Hoover came to see James D. Reid, who'd written a book about the telegraph.

Hoover said, "I manage a Western Union office in Pennsylvania. Our telegraph operators want to celebrate Samuel Morse's eightieth birthday."

"How?" Reid asked.

"We'd like to put up a statue of Morse in Central Park in New York."

"It will be expensive," Reid said.

Robert Hoover said, "The expense will be shared

by thousands of telegraph operators. After all, they owe their livelihood to Morse. They want to honor the person who made their profession possible.''

With Reid's help, telegraphers from all over North America sent in their contributions—a dollar from each telegraph operator and twenty-five cents from each messenger.

But some people objected to a statue to a living person. ''Would it be right?'' they asked.

''Do not worry,'' James Reid told them. ''I can think of no one who is less likely to let the honor go to his head.''

On the pleasant afternoon of June 10, 1871, thousands of telegraph operators strolled into Central Park. They gathered on a knoll where star-and-stripe bunting covered the bronze statue.

Samuel Morse decided it would not be proper to attend the statue unveiling. But his daughter, Leila, did attend. Theodore Roosevelt, Sr., escorted her.

After a time of speech making, William Orton, president of Western Union, mounted the platform by the statue. He pulled the cord. The flag fell away to reveal the larger-than-life figure of Morse in bronze. The band played and the crowd cheered.

The ceremony concluded with the park ringing to the sound of the hymn ''Praise God from Whom All Blessings Flow.''

Samuel Morse did want to meet his ''children.'' He held a reception that night at the Music Hall on Fourteenth Street.

The telegraphers, too, looked forward to catching a glimpse of their hero. They quickly filled the Music Hall. On a table in the middle of the stage was an old-fashioned telegraph sender, identical to the one used to send the first message twenty-seven years earlier.

MORSE

Cyrus Field, Horace Greeley, Henry Ward Beecher, and William Orton waited on the stage. Annie Ellsworth came, too, as a special guest.

Samuel Morse walked onto the stage. A wave of excitement passed through the crowd. Samuel Morse! Tall, graceful, white hair, white beard—but alert. His kindly blue eyes sparkled with the excitement of the moment.

Samuel took the seat of honor. The master of ceremonies presented him with a roll of paper more than nineteen feet long. It contained the names of his "children" who contributed to the statue.

At nine o'clock, William Orton cut short the speeches and stepped to the ancient telegraph. The machine still worked. In fact, it would be used tonight.

William Orton explained, "The telegraph wires are open to every city in the United States and Canada," he said. "Miss Sadie E. Cornwell will send Professor Morse's message. Then he will take the keyboard."

Miss Cornwell accepted the sheet of paper from Samuel Morse. The hall fell silent. She tapped out the message. The hall of telegraphers could understand it by "ear," by listening to the clicks.

Miss Cornwell stood aside for Morse to take her place. Breathlessly, the throng watched as his finger touched the key.

Samuel Morse's message said, "Greetings and thanks to the telegraph fraternity throughout the world. Glory to God in the highest, on earth peace, good will to men."

He struck the final letters. "S. F. B. Morse."

Samuel's hand fell from the key. The entire audience jumped to their feet and burst into a wild storm of deafening cheers.

Samuel Morse looked around the hall at the young faces. Many of them had not even been born when he sent that first message more than a quarter century earlier.

In the fall of 1871, Samuel Morse left his beloved Locust Grove to spend the winter in New York.

As the carriage passed through the gate on the way out, Samuel said, "Stop here a moment, driver." Samuel stood up in the open wagon. Fondly, he looked back along the wooded drive, through the trees, and over the sunlighted lawn to his old house.

"Beautiful! Beautiful!" Samuel said. In a whisper he added, "But I have prepared a place elsewhere."

During his lifetime, Samuel enjoyed excellent health. He'd been confined in bed only once, because of a broken leg. In the spring of 1872, however, he grew weak. He spent more of his time inside.

His New York pastor, William Adams, called on him at his house on Twenty-Second Street. The pastor found Samuel in bed reading the Bible.

Morse closed his Bible. "I love to study the Guide Book of the country to which I am going," he told Pastor Adams. "The world, with all of its attractions, I find is losing its hold upon me."

"God has blessed your life," Pastor Adams said.

"Yes," Samuel said. Cheerfully he added, "And the best is yet to come."

Samuel grew weaker during the night. Pneumonia set in. The next day one of the doctors attending him listened to his lungs. The doctor tapped his chest. "This is the way we doctors telegraph," the physician said.

A momentary gleam of humor lighted Samuel's eyes. "Very good," he whispered.

A few hours later the telegraph lines carried the mournful news. On April 2, 1872, Samuel F. B. Morse had died.

15

Samuel F. B. Morse in Today's World

Samuel F. B. Morse met with great fame during his lifetime. Nearly every country in the world gave him a medal or some other award. After his death, he was elected to the Hall of Fame of Great Americans.

The telegraph is today considered one of the ten most important inventions of all time. It was the first invention to put electricity to practical use.

But even without the telegraph, Samuel F. B. Morse would still be an important figure in American history.

The father of the telegraph is also the father of photography in America. After the success of the daguerreotype portraits, photographers asked for his expert opinion in photographic matters. His knowledge of art, composition, and the photographic process made him the logical choice to judge competitions among photographers, and he did so on numerous occasions.

Samuel F. B. Morse came from a remarkable family. His father wrote *Geography Made Easy*, the first geography book for the United States. His grandfather served as president of Harvard. Samuel and his brother Sidney invented and patented a marble-cutting machine and an improved water pump. Together the three brothers began several journals, including the New York *Observer* and the *Journal of Commerce.*

As a young man, Samuel Morse set out to be an artist. By age forty-one he'd gained world wide recognition for his painting. He painted three hundred major canvases and numerous sketches which today hang in art museums and private collections. His painting *Gallery of the Louvre* recently sold for more than three million dollars, the highest price ever paid up to that time for a painting by an American artist.

He also helped found a school of painting called "Democratic Art." The purpose of this type of painting is to educate the public mind and turn people's thoughts to moral principles. His *Representative Hall* is one example of a painting that shows democracy in action.

Morse also began the National Academy of Design. He served as its president for many years.

But Morse was not merely an artist or a man of science. He was a man of God. His life cannot be separated from his religious devotion.

He took a leading role in the establishment of Sunday schools. With missionary zeal he constantly urged others to the faith. He freely gave to missionaries, to religious institutions, and to schools that trained ministers.

He believed in education—but of the proper kind. According to Morse, "Education without religion is in danger of substituting wild theories for the simple commonsense rules of Christianity."

When asked to sum up his life, Samuel said, ''I agree with that sentence of Annie Ellsworth, 'What hath God wrought!' It is *His* work. 'Not unto us, but to Thy name, O Lord, be all the praise.' ''

BIBLIOGRAPHY

Isaac Asimov, *Asimov's Biographical Encyclopedia of Science and Technology* (Garden City: Doubleday & Company, Inc., 1972).

Henry M. Field, *The Story of the American Telegraph* (New York: Charles Scribners & Sons, 1893).

John F. Fulton and Elizabeth H. Thompson, *Benjamin Silliman, Pathfinder in American Science* (New York: Abelard-Schuman, 1947).

Wilma Pitchford Hays, *Samuel Morse and the Telegraph* (New York: Franklin Watts, Inc., 1960).

Oliver W. Larkin, *Samuel F. B. Morse and American Democratic Art* (Boston: Little, Brown and Com- pany, 1954).

Jean Lee Latham, *Medals For Morse* (New York: Aladdin Books, 1954).

Carleton Mabee, *The American Leonardo: A Life of Samuel F. B. Morse* (New York: Alfred A. Knoff, 1943).

Irwin Math, *Morse, Marconi and You* (New York: Charles Scribner's Sons, 1979).

Edward Lind Morse, Editor, *Samuel F. B. Morse, His Letters and Journals, (2 vol.)* (New York: Houghton Mifflin Company, 1914; reprint edition Da Capo Press, New York, 1973).

Beaumont Newhall, *The History of Photography from 1839 to the Present Day* (New York: The Museum of Modern Art, 1949).

Beaumont Newhall, *Latent Image* (Garden City: Doubleday & Company, Inc., 1967).

Samuel I. Prime, *The Life of Samuel F. B. Morse* (New York: D. Appleton and Company, 1875).

James D. Reid, *The Telegraph in America* (New York: Derby Bros., 1879; reprint edition Arno Press, New York, 1974).

Dorothea J. Snow, *Samuel Morse Inquisitive Boy* (New York: Bobbs-Merrill Company, Inc., 1950).

Robert L. Thompson, *Wiring a Continent* (Princeton, New Jersey: Princeton University Press, 1947; reprint edition Arno Press, New York, 1972).

INDEX

SOWERS SERIES

0 143